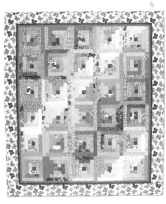

MW00604063

Roosters in the Morning

pieced by Lanelle Herron
quilted by Sue Needle

In the country, every day begins with crowing roosters greeting the sun. Whimsical and full of fun, this quilt is perfect for the young at heart.

A group of roosters or a flock of birds fly right into place on this adorable strip quilt.

FABRIC USED: "Nest" by Tula Pink

instructions on pages 26 - 35

Flying Birds

pieced by Edna Summers

Soft sculptures add a designer touch that will complete and complement your room decor. Use up your 10" scraps and create a fun flock of little birds.

Hang them from ribbons or fill a basket for a lovely table centerpiece.

FABRIC USED: "Nest" by Tula Pink

instructions on page 45

Scroll Birds

pieced by Kayleen Allen
appliqued by Janice Irick
quilted by Julie Lawson

Let your imagination take flight! A roosting brood of little birds has been surrounded by a flock of flying geese on a quilt that would be fun to make in any color palette.

I used my leftovers from the 'Layer Cake' for the Bluebirds Quilt on page 6 to make this quilt.

FABRIC USED: "Nest" by Tula Pink

instructions on pages 36 - 39

Bluebirds Quilt

pieced by Edna Summers
quilted by Julie Lawson

Bluebirds come home to roost on this gorgeously simple quilt. Large blocks display a collection of coordinated fabrics, making this a perfect choice for using leftover squares from your personal stash.

Simple applique shapes and easy embroidery add a special touch to the finished quilt.

FABRIC USED: "Nest" by Tula Pink

instructions on pages 40 - 43

Bluebird Pillow

Always popular, accent pillows soften the spaces in a home. This easy applique will be a treasured gift and can be made quickly from leftovers for a lovely designer look without the designer price.

Round & Round

pieced by Donna Arends Hansen
quilted by Sue Needle

You'll enjoy your morning coffee or evening tea even more when snuggled in your favorite chair with this cozy, fun-filled quilt. Printed fabrics in a mocha theme present cups, coffee pots, saucers, and some really lively tile patterns giving this quilt a motion that goes Round and Round.

FABRIC USED: "Bistro" by Deb Strain

instructions on pages 46 - 53

Striped Pinwheels

pieced by Donna Perrotta
quilted by Sue Needle

*Spicy cinnamon, hot chocolate and peppermint
sticks! Create a fragrant medley of delicious color
with quick pieced blocks that are a joy to cook up.
Season to taste with a lovely pieced border and you
have a fabulous quilt your family will love.*

FABRIC USED: "Cotton Blossoms"
by Bonnie of Cotton Way

instructions on pages 54 - 56

Rainbow of Colors

pieced by Donna Perrotta
quilted by Julie Lawson

Sunlight spills into rainbows of color playfully captured in cloth. This delightful quilt lights up any room with its happy colors and charming motifs.

Perfect for every child and child-at-heart, this log cabin will be a family favorite.

FABRIC USED: "Butterfly Fling" by Me & My Sister

instructions on pages 57 - 61

Stairway to Heaven

pieced by Betty Nowlin
quilted by Sue Needle

Create an exciting and unusual graphic quilt in an afternoon. Large blocks make it easy, color placement makes it stunning!

This design works beautifully in any color palette and is a fabulous quick or beginner project.

FABRIC USED: "Urban Couture" by Basic Grey

instructions on pages 62 - 63

Five Friends

pieced by Kayleen Allen
quilted by Sue Needle
Americana at its best, this grass-roots
design deserves a five star rating. Pinks, choco-
late browns and indigo blues capture the color
palette of the 1800's, taking us back to a time
when quilts were not a luxury item.

FABRIC: "Civil War Crossing" by Barbara Brackman

instructions on pages 64 - 71

Kaleidoscope of Color

*pieced by
Donna Arends Hansen
quilted by Sue Needle*

Capture the ever-changing fractured color of a kaleidoscope with this gorgeous design. Simple half-square triangles create the effect of fascinating color on a quilt that entertains your eye with splashes of pattern.

FABRIC USED:
"Charisma" by Chez Moi

instructions on pages 72 - 75

Small Kaleidoscope

*pieced by Donna Kinsey
quilted by Sue Needle*

A perfect small project. This small kaleidoscope uses the leftovers from the large kaleidoscope quilt.

It's a lovely complement for your decor.

instructions on pages 76 - 77

Quilt without applique.

Fresh Picked Peas

pieced by Betty Nowlin
quilted by Sue Needle

Invigorate your creative spirit with the irresistible aromas and scrumptious sights of the vegetable garden: pungent mint, lettuce leaves glistening with dewdrops, and the mouthwatering flavor of fresh picked peas.

Immerse yourself in a lush garden and blue skies that invite you to enjoy the flavors of summer as you create this fabulous quilt.

FABRIC USED: "Charisma" by Chez Moi

instructions on page 19 - 21

Fresh Picked Peas

photo is on page 18

SIZE: 50" x 64"
TIP: Add more borders to make a larger quilt.

YARDAGE:
Yardage is given for using either fabric yardage or
   'Layer Cake' squares.
We used a *Moda* "Charisma" by Chez Moi
   'Layer Cake' collection of 10" x 10" fabric squares
   - we purchased 1 'Layer Cake'

5 squares	OR	⅝ yard Light Blue
4 squares	OR	⅓ yard Medium Blue
5 squares	OR	⅝ yard Green
2 squares	OR	⅓ yard Blue-Green
2 squares	OR	⅓ yard Stripe
1 square	OR	⅓ Brown (applique)
2 squares	OR	⅓ Ivory (applique)

Border #1 & Sashing	Purchase ⅔ yard Green solid
Border #2 & Binding	Purchase 1⅝ yards Green print
Backing	Purchase 3 yards
Batting	Purchase 58" x 72"

Sewing machine, needle, thread

Optional Embroidery: *DMC* Dark Green pearl cotton or floss
#22 or #24 Chenille needle

PREPARATION FOR SQUARES:
   Cut all squares 10" x 10".
   Label the stacks or pieces as you cut.

SORTING:
   Sort the following 10" x 10" squares into stacks:

POSITION	QUANTITY	& COLOR
1, 3, 8, 10	4	Light Blue
2, 6, 7, 9, 12	5	Green
4, 5, 11, 14	4	Medium Blue
13, 16	1	Blue-Green
15	1	Stripe

CUTTING:
   Cut 16 Green sashing strips 4" x 10".

SEW BLOCKS:
   Refer to the Quilt Assembly Diagram for block
numbers and position of the sashings.

For odd numbered blocks, sew a sashing strip to the bottom of the square.

For even numbered blocks, sew a sashing strip to the top of the square.

Each block will measure 10" x 13½" at this point.

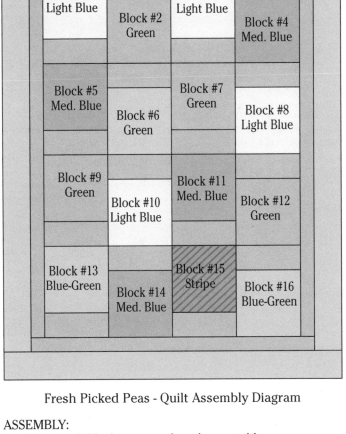

Fresh Picked Peas - Quilt Assembly Diagram

ASSEMBLY:
   Arrange all blocks on a work surface or table.
   Refer to diagram for block placement and direction.
   Sew blocks together in 4 rows, 4 blocks per row. Press.
   Sew rows together. Press.

Border #1:
Cut strips 2½" by the width of fabric.
Sew strips together end to end.
   Cut 2 strips 2½" x 52½" for sides.
   Cut 2 strips 2½" x 42½" for top and bottom.
   Sew side borders to the quilt. Press.
   Sew top and bottom borders to the quilt. Press.

Border #2:
Cut strips 4½" wide parallel to the selvage to eliminate piecing.
   Cut 2 strips 4½" x 56½" for sides.
   Cut 2 strips 4½" x 50½" for top and bottom.
   Sew side borders to the quilt. Press.
   Sew top and bottom borders to the quilt. Press.

APPLIQUE:
   Refer to Applique instructions.
   Cut out patterns from leftover squares.
   Applique as desired.
   Embroider stems with a long and short Running Stitch.

FINISHING:
Quilting: See Basic Instructions.
Binding: Cut strips 2½" wide.
      Sew together end to end to equal 238".
      See Binding Instructions.

Refer to Basic Applique instructions

Add a scant ¹/₄" around the edge of each piece
for turned applique

Bunny
Cut 1 Ivory

Add a scant ¹/₄"
around the edge for
turned applique

Bunny
Cut 1 Ivory

Add a scant ¹/₄"
around the edge for
turned applique

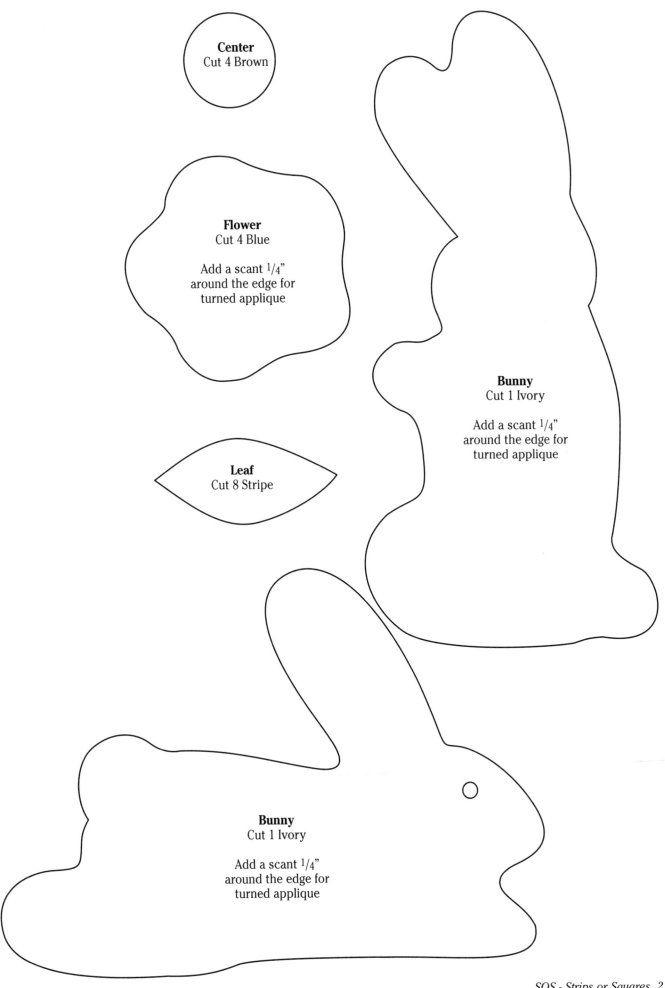

Center
Cut 4 Brown

Flower
Cut 4 Blue

Add a scant 1/4"
around the edge for
turned applique

Bunny
Cut 1 Ivory

Add a scant 1/4"
around the edge for
turned applique

Leaf
Cut 8 Stripe

Bunny
Cut 1 Ivory

Add a scant 1/4"
around the edge for
turned applique

The Best Things About
'Jelly Rolls' and 'Layer Cakes'

I love to quilt, but it is often difficult to find time to cut and piece a quilt top. When I saw collections of 2¹/₂" pre-cut fabric strips and the selections of 10" pre-cut squares, I knew they were the answer.

No more spending hours choosing and cutting fabrics. Now I can begin sewing right away. Beautiful colors are available in every set. So whether I like jewel colors, heritage patterns, soft pastels or earthy tones... there is an assortment for me.

Now my goals... a handmade cover for every bed, an heirloom quilt for each new baby and a pieced quilt for each of my children... are within reach. With 'Jelly Rolls' and 'Layer Cakes' it is possible to complete a quilt top in a weekend.

After I piece all the blocks together, I use leftover strips for the borders and binding. Nothing really goes to waste and, if needed, I can purchase a bit of extra fabric for an extra punch of color or an additional yard for the border.

TIP: Quantities are given in strips or squares and yardage so you know what you need and can start right away.

Tips for Working with Strips

Guide for Yardage:

2¹/₂" Strips - Each ¼ yard or a 'Fat Quarter' equals 3 strips - A pre-cut 'Jelly Roll' strip is 2½" x 44"

10" x 10" Squares - Four 10" squares can be cut from ⅓ yard or eight 10" squares can be cut from ⅝ yard.

Pre-cut strips are cut on the crosswise grain and are prone to stretching. These tips will help reduce stretching and make your quilt lay flat for quilting.

1. If you are cutting yardage, cut on the grain. Cut fat quarters on grain, parallel to the 18" side.

2. When sewing crosswise grain strips together, take care not to stretch the strips. If you detect any puckering as you go, rip out the seam and sew it again.

3. Press, Do Not Iron. Carefully open fabric, with the seam to one side, press without moving the iron. A back-and-forth ironing motion stretches the fabric.

4. Reduce the wiggle in your borders with this technique from garment making. First, accurately cut your borders to the exact measure of the quilt top. Then, before sewing the border to the quilt, run a double row of stay stitches along the outside edge to maintain the original shape and prevent stretching. Pin the border to the quilt, taking care not to stretch the quilt top to make it fit. Pinning reduces slipping and stretching.

Rotary Cutting

Rotary Cutter: Friend or Foe

A rotary cutter is wonderful and useful. When not used correctly, the sharp blade can be a dangerous tool. Follow these safety tips:

1. Never cut toward you.

2. Use a sharp blade. Pressing harder on a dull blade can cause the blade to jump the ruler and injure your fingers.

3. Always disengage the blade before the cutter leaves your hand, even if you intend to pick it up immediately.

Rotary cutters have been caught when lifting fabric, have fallen onto the floor and have cut fingers.

Basic Sewing

You now have precisely cut strips that are exactly the correct width. You are well on your way to blocks that fit together perfectly. Accurate sewing is the next important step.

Matching Edges:

1. Carefully line up the edges of your strips. Many times, if the underside is off a little, your seam will be off by ⅛". This does not sound like much until you have 8 seams in a block, each off by ⅛". Now your finished block is a whole inch wrong!

2. Pin the pieces together to prevent them shifting.

Seam Allowance:

I cannot stress enough the importance of accurate ¼" seams. All the quilts in this book are measured for ¼" seams unless otherwise indicated.

Most sewing machine manufacturers offer a Quarter-inch foot. A Quarter-inch foot is the most worthwhile investment you can make in your quilting.

Pressing:

I want to talk about pressing even before we get to sewing because proper pressing can make the difference between a quilt that wins a ribbon at the quilt show and one that does not.

Press, do NOT iron. What does that mean? Many of us want to move the iron back and forth along the seam. This "ironing" stretches the strip out of shape and creates errors that accumulate as the quilt is constructed. Believe it or not, there is a correct way to press your seams, and here it is:

1. Do NOT use steam with your iron. If you need a little water, spritz it on.

2. Place your fabric flat on the ironing board without opening the seam. Set a hot iron on the seam and count to 3. Lift the iron and move to the next position along the seam. Repeat until the entire seam is pressed. This sets and sinks the threads into the fabric.

3. Now, carefully lift the top strip and fold it away from you so the seam is on one side. Usually the seam is pressed toward the darker fabric, but often the direction of the seam is determined by the piecing requirements.

4. Press the seam open with your fingers. Add a little water or spray starch if it wants to close again. Lift the iron and place it on the seam. Count to 3. Lift the iron again and continue until the seam is pressed. Do NOT use the tip of the iron to push the seam open. So many people do this and wonder later why their blocks are not fitting together.

5. Most critical of all: For accuracy every seam must be pressed before the next seam is sewn.

Working with 'Crosswise Grain' Strips:

Strips cut on the crosswise grain (from selvage to selvage) have problems similar to bias edges and are prone to stretching. To reduce stretching and make your quilt lay flat for quilting, keep these tips in mind.

1. Take care not to stretch the strips as you sew.

2. Adjust the sewing thread tension and the presser foot pressure if needed.

3. If you detect any puckering as you go, rip out the seam and sew it again. It is much easier to take out a seam now than to do it after the block is sewn.

Sewing Bias Edges:

Bias edges wiggle and stretch out of shape very easily. They are not recommended for beginners, but even a novice can accomplish bias edges if these techniques are employed.

1. Stabilize the bias edge with one of these methods:

   a) Press with spray starch.

   b) Press freezer paper or removable iron-on stabilizer to the back of the fabric.

   c) Sew a double row of stay stitches along the bias edge and ⅛" from the bias edge. This is a favorite technique of garment makers.

2. Pin, pin, pin! I know many of us dislike pinning, but when working with bias edges, pinning makes the difference between intersections that match and those that do not.

Building Better Borders:

Wiggly borders make a quilt very difficult to finish. However, wiggly borders can be avoided with these techniques.

1. Cut the borders on grain. That means cutting your strips parallel to the selvage edge.

2. Accurately cut your borders to the exact measure of the quilt.

3. If your borders are piece stripped from crosswise grain fabrics, press well with spray starch and sew a double row of stay stitches along the outside edge to maintain the original shape and prevent stretching.

4. Pin the border to the quilt, taking care not to stretch the quilt top to make it fit. Pinning reduces slipping and stretching.

Embroidery Use 24" lengths of doubled pearl cotton or 6-ply floss and a #22 or #24 Chenille needle (this needle has a large eye). Outline large elements.

Running Stitch Come up at A. Weave the needle through the fabric, making LONG stitches on the top and SHORT stitches on the bottom. Keep stitches even.

Applique Instructions

Basic Turned Edge

1. Trace pattern onto no-melt template plastic (or onto Wash-Away Tear-Away Stabilizer).

2. Cut out the fabric shape leaving a scant $1/4$" fabric border all around and clip the curves.

3. **Plastic Template Method -** Place plastic shape on the wrong side of the fabric. Spray edges with starch. Press a $1/4$" border over the edge of the template plastic with the tip of a hot iron. Press firmly.

   Stabilizer Method - Place stabilizer shape on the wrong side of the fabric. Use a glue stick to press a $1/4$" border over the edge of the stabilizer securing it with the glue stick. Press firmly.

5. Remove the template, maintaining the folded edge on the back of the fabric.

6. Position the shape on the quilt and Blindstitch in place.

Basic Turned Edge by Hand

1. Cut out the shape leaving a $1/4$" fabric border all around.

2. Baste the shapes to the quilt, keeping the basting stitches away from the edge of the fabric.

3. Begin with all areas that are under other layers and work to the topmost layer.

4. For an area no more than 2" ahead of where you are working, trim to $1/8$" and clip the curves.

5. Using the needle, roll the edge under and sew tiny Blindstitches to secure.

Using Fusible Web for Iron-on Applique:

1. Trace pattern onto Steam a Seam 2 fusible web.

2. Press the patterns onto the wrong side of fabric.

3. Cut out patterns exactly on the drawn line.

4. Score web paper with a pin, then remove the paper.

5. Position the fabric, fusible side down, on the quilt. Press with a hot iron following the fusible web manufacturer's instructions.

6. Stitch around the edge by hand.

Optional: Stabilize the wrong side of the fabric with your favorite stabilizer.

Use a size 80 machine embroidery needle. Fill the bobbin with lightweight basting thread and thread machine with machine embroidery thread that complements the color being appliqued.

Set your machine for a Zigzag stitch and adjust the thread tension if needed. Use a scrap to experiment with different stitch widths and lengths until you find the one you like best.

Sew slowly.

Basic Layering Instructions

Marking Your Quilt:

If you choose to mark your quilt for hand or machine quilting, it is much easier to do so before layering. Press your quilt before you begin. Here are some handy tips regarding marking.

1. A disappearing pen may vanish before you finish.

2. Use a White pencil on dark fabrics.

3. If using a washable Blue pen, remember that pressing may make the pen permanent.

Pieced Backings:

1. Press the backing fabric before measuring.

2. If possible cut backing fabrics on grain, parallel to the selvage edges.

3. Piece 3 parts rather than 2 whenever possible, sewing 2 side borders to the center. This reduces stress on the pieced seam.

4. Backing and batting should extend at least 2" on each side of the quilt.

Creating a Quilt Sandwich:

1. Press the backing and top to remove all wrinkles.

2. Lay the backing wrong side up on the table.

3. Position the batting over the backing and smooth out all wrinkles.

4. Center the quilt top over the batting leaving a 2" border all around.

5. Pin the layers together with 2" safety pins positioned a handwidth apart. A grapefruit spoon makes inserting the pins easier. Leaving the pins open in the container speeds up the basting on the next quilt.

Basic Quilting Instructions

Hand Quilting:

Many quilters enjoy the serenity of hand quilting. Because the quilt is handled a great deal, it is important to securely baste the sandwich together. Place the quilt in a hoop and don't forget to hide your knots.

Machine Quilting:

All the quilts in this book were machine quilted. Some were quilted on a large, free-arm quilting machine and others were quilted on a sewing machine. If you have never machine quilted before, practice on some scraps first.

Straight Line Machine Quilting Tips:

1. Pin baste the layers securely.

2. Set up your sewing machine with a size 80 quilting needle and a walking foot.

3. Experimenting with the decorative stitches on your machine adds interest to your quilt. You do not have to quilt the entire piece with the same stitch. Variety is the spice of life, so have fun trying out stitches you have never used before as well as your favorite stand-bys.

Free Motion Machine Quilting Tips:

1. Pin baste the layers securely.

2. Set up your sewing machine with a spring needle, a quilting foot, and lower the feed dogs.

Basic Mitered Binding

A Perfect Finish:

The binding endures the most stress on a quilt and is usually the first thing to wear out. For this reason, we recommend using a double fold binding.

1. Trim the backing and batting even with the quilt edge.

2. If possible cut strips on the crosswise grain because a little bias in the binding is a Good thing. This is the only place in the quilt where bias is helpful, for it allows the binding to give as it is turned to the back and sewn in place.

3. Strips are usually cut 2½" wide, but check the instructions for your project before cutting.

4. Sew strips end to end to make a long strip sufficient to go all around the quilt plus 4"- 6".

5. With wrong sides together, fold the strip in half lengthwise. Press.

6. Stretch out your hand and place your little finger at the corner of the quilt top. Place the binding where your thumb touches the edge of the quilt. Aligning the edge of the quilt with the raw edges of the binding, pin the binding in place along the first side.

7. Leaving a 2" tail for later use, begin sewing the binding to the quilt with a ¼" seam.

For Mitered Corners:

1. Stop ¼" from the first corner. Leave the needle in the quilt and turn it 90°. Hit the reverse button on your machine and back off the quilt leaving the threads connected.

2. Fold the binding perpendicular to the side you sewed, making a 45° angle. Carefully maintaining the first fold, bring the binding back along the edge to be sewn.

3. Carefully align the edges of the binding with the quilt edge and sew as you did the first side. Repeat this process until you reach the tail left at the beginning. Fold the tail out of the way and sew until you are ¼" from the beginning stitches.

4. Remove the quilt from the machine. Fold the quilt out of the way and match the binding tails together. Carefully sew the binding tails with a ¼" seam. You can do this by hand if you prefer.

Finishing the Binding:

5. Trim the seam to reduce bulk.

6. Finish stitching the binding to the quilt across the join you just sewed.

7. Turn the binding to the back of the quilt. To reduce bulk at the corners, fold the miter in the opposite direction from which it was folded on the front.

8. Hand-sew a Blind stitch on the back of the quilt to secure the binding in place.

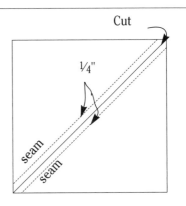

Half-Square Triangle

1. Place 2 squares right sides together.
2. Draw a diagonal line from corner to corner.
3. Stitch ¼" on each side of the line.
4. Cut squares apart on the diagonal line.
5. Open the 2 new squares with 2 colors.
6. Press. Trim off dog-ears.
7. Center and trim to size.

Align the raw edge of the binding with the raw edge of the quilt top. Start about 8" from the corner and go along the first side with a ¼" seam.

Stop ¼" from the edge. Then stitch a slant to the corner (through both layers of binding)... lift up, then down, as you line up the edge. Fold the binding back.

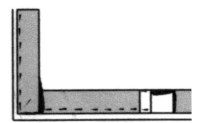

Align the raw edge again. Continue stitching the next side with a ¼" seam as you sew the binding in place.

Roosters in the Morning

photo is on page 4

SIZE: 66" x 72"
TIP: Add more borders to make a larger quilt.

YARDAGE:
Yardage is given for using either fabric yardage or
   'Jelly Roll' strips.
We used a *Moda* "Nest" by Tula Pink
   'Jelly Roll' collection of 2½" fabric strips
   - we purchased 1 'Jelly Roll'

9 strips	OR	⅔ yard Turquoise
9 strips	OR	⅔ yard Green
2 strips	OR	⅙ yard Brown
5 strips	OR	⅜ yard Red
3 strips	OR	¼ yard Dark Red
2 strips	OR	⅙ yard Gold
2 strips	OR	⅙ yard Gold & Brown

Block Background	Purchase 1⅔ yard White
Border #3 & Binding	Purchase 1⅞ yards print
Backing	Purchase 4 yards
Batting	Purchase 74" x 80"

6 Black ⅝" buttons for eyes
Sewing machine, needle, thread

PREPARATION FOR STRIPS:
   Cut all strips 2½" by the width of fabric
      (usually 42" - 44").
   Cut the longest strips first.
   Label the stacks or pieces as you cut.

SORTING:
   Sort the following 2½" strips into stacks:

POSITION	QUANTITY & COLOR
Roosters	5 Red
Roosters	2 Brown
Roosters	2 Dark Red
Roosters	2 Gold

TIP: LABEL THE PIECES AS YOU CUT.

SASHING:
Cut the sashing strips first. Save them until
you need them to assemble the quilt.

VERTICAL SASHING STRIPS:
CUTTING CHART

Color	Quantity	Length	Position
Green	4	28½"	Sash K, M, R, S
Turquoise	4	28½"	Sash J, L, Q, T

HORIZONTAL SASHING STRIPS:
CUTTING CHART

Color	Quantity	Length	Position
White print yardage	2	9"	Sash W
Gold & Brown	6	14½"	Sash A, D, G, N, O, P
Turquoise	3	14½"	Sash C, F, H
Green	3	14½"	Sash B, E, I

Basic Techniques

Snowball Corner Diagram

SNOWBALL CORNERS:

Several strips in each block use the Snowball Corner technique. The direction of the diagonal for each strip in the block varies, so you must carefully note the diagonal on the block assembly diagram. Some strips have a corner on only one end. The squares used as Snowball Corners are labelled with a "c" in the cutting list.

Tip: Fold back the triangle and check its position before you sew.

Align a square with the appropriate end of the strip and sew on the diagonal line. Fold the triangle back and press before attaching it to any other strips.

LEGS FOR ROOSTERS:

Make 2

All legs are made the same... but they are different lengths. Make all the legs at one time to make piecing faster.

Use 2 Brown 32" strips. Cut them in half lengthwise to make 4 narrow Brown strips for the legs, each 1" x 32".

Cut 2 strips 1½" x 32" from White yardage.

Sew strips together side by side, Brown-White-Brown. Make 2 units 2½" x 32".

Cut the long units into 6 leg units. (Rooster A -6½", B-8½", C-10½", D-8½", E-10½", F-8½").

 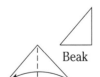

Beak

BIRD BEAK:

For each beak, cut a Red or Yellow 1½" square and fold it 3 or 4 times into the desired beak shape.

Position in the seam and stitch in place.

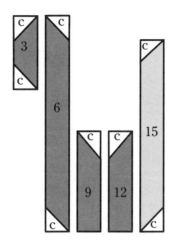

5 Special Shaped Strips

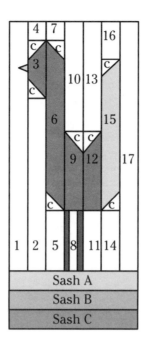

Sash A

Sash B

Sash C

BLOCK A:

CUTTING CHART

Color	Quantity	Length	Position
White yardage	2	26½"	#1, 17
	1	18½"	#2
	2	12½"	#10, 13
	3	6½"	#5, 11, 14
	1	4½"	#16
	10	2½"	#4, 7, "c"
Dark Red	1	18½"	#6
	2	8½"	#9, 12
	1	6½"	#3
Red	1	16½"	#15
Leg Unit	1	2½" x 6½"	#8

BLOCK A ASSEMBLY:

Snowball Corners:

You need #3, 6, 9, 12 & 15 and 8 White squares.
Refer to the Snowball Corners diagram on page 1.
Carefully note the direction of each diagonal.

#3, 6 & 15: Align a White square with both ends.

#9 & 12: Align a White square with 1 end.
Draw the diagonals and sew on the line.
Fold back the flaps and press.

Assembly: Arrange the pieces on a work surface or table.

Column 1: #1
Column 2: Sew 2-3-4. Press.
Column 3: Sew 5-6-7. Press.
Column 4: Sew 8-9-10. Press.
Column 5: Sew 11-12-13. Press.
Column 6: Sew 14-15-16. Press.
Column 7: #17

Sew the columns together. Press.
Sew Sashes A, B, and C to the bottom of the piece. Press.

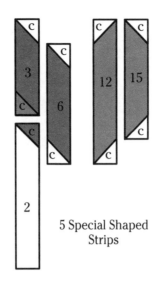

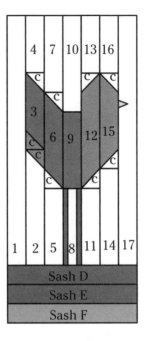

5 Special Shaped Strips

BLOCK B:

CUTTING CHART

Color	Quantity	Length	Position
White yardage	2	26½"	#1, 17
	1	12½"	#2
	2	10½"	#10, 14
	3	8½"	#5, 7, 11
	3	6½"	#4, 13, 16
	7	2½"	"c"
Dark Red	1	10½"	#6
	2	8½"	#3, 9
Red	1	12½"	#12
	1	10½"	#15
	2	2½"	#2c, 3c
Leg Unit	1	2½" x 8½"	#8

BLOCK B ASSEMBLY:

Snowball Corners:

  You need #2, 3, 6, 12 & 15 and 7 White and 2 Red squares.
  Refer to the Snowball Corners diagram on page 1.
  Carefully note the color and direction of each diagonal.

#6, 12 & 15: Align a White square with both ends.

#3: Align a White square with 1 end and a Red square with the other.

#2: Align a Red square with 1 end.
  Draw the diagonals and sew on the line.
  Fold back the flap and press.

Assembly: Arrange the pieces on a work surface or table.
  Column 1: #1
  Column 2: Sew 2-3-4. Press.
  Column 3: Sew 5-6-7. Press.
  Column 4: Sew 8-9-10. Press.
  Column 5: Sew 11-12-13. Press.
  Column 6: Sew 14-15-16. Press.
  Column 7: #17
Sew the columns together. Press.
Sew Sashes D, E, and F to the bottom of the piece. Press.

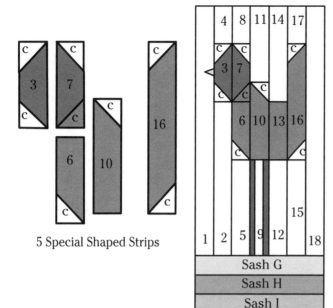

5 Special Shaped Strips

BLOCK C:

CUTTING CHART

Color	Quantity	Length	Position
White yardage	2	26½"	#1,18
	1	16½"	#2
	4	10½"	#5, 12, 14, 15
	1	8½"	#11
	3	4½"	#4, 8, 17
	7	2½"	"c"
Dark Red	2	6½"	#3, 7
Red	1	12½"	#16
	2	6½"	#6, 13
	1	2½"	#6c
Leg Unit	1	2½" x 10½"	#9

BLOCK C ASSEMBLY:

Snowball Corners:

    You need #3, 6, 7, 10, & 16.
        You also need 7 White squares and 1 Red square.
    Refer to the Snowball Corners diagram.
    Carefully note the direction of each diagonal.
#3 & 16: Align a White square with both ends.
#6 & 10: Align a White square with 1 end.
#7: Align a White square with 1 end and a Red square on the other.
    Draw the diagonals and sew on the line.
    Fold back the flap and press.

Assembly: Arrange the pieces on a work surface or table.
Column 1: #1
Column 2: Sew 2-3-4. Press.
Column 3: Sew 5-6-7-8. Press.
Column 4: Sew 9-10-11. Press.
Column 5: Sew 12-13-14. Press.
Column 6: Sew 15-16-17. Press.
Column 7: #18
Sew the columns together. Press.
Sew Sashes G, H, and I to the bottom of the piece. Press.

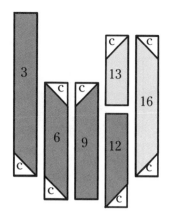

6 Special Shaped Strips

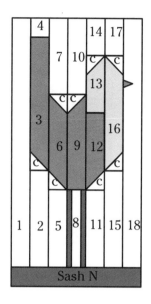

BLOCK D:

CUTTING CHART

Color	Quantity	Length	Position
White yardage	2	26½"	#1, 18
	2	10½"	#2, 15
	4	8½"	#5, 7, 10, 11
	2	4½"	#14, 17
	9	2½"	#4, "c"
Red	1	14½"	#3
	2	10½"	#6, #9
	1	8½"	#12
Gold	1	12½"	#16
	1	6½"	#13
Leg Unit	1	2½" x 8½"	#8

BLOCK D ASSEMBLY:

Snowball Corners:
> You need #3, 6, 9, 12, 13, & 16 and 8 White squares.
> Refer to the Snowball Corners diagram.
> Carefully note the direction of each diagonal.

#6 & 16: Align a White square with both ends of each strip.

#3, 9, 12, & 13: Align a White square on one end only.
> Draw the diagonals and sew on the line.
> Fold back the flap and press.

Assembly: Arrange the pieces on a work surface or table.
> Column 1: #1
> Column 2: Sew 2-3-4. Press.
> Column 3: Sew 5-6-7. Press.
> Column 4: Sew 8-9-10. Press.
> Column 5: Sew 11-12-13-14. Press.
> Column 6: Sew 15-16-17. Press.
> Column 7: #18

Sew the columns together. Press.

Sew Sash N to the bottom of the piece. Press.

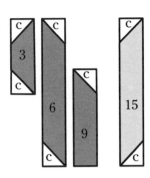

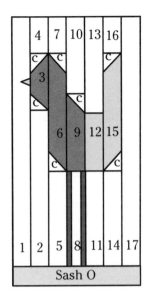

4 Special Shaped Strips

BLOCK E:

CUTTING CHART

Color	Quantity	Length	Position
White yardage	2	26½"	#1, 17
	1	16½"	#2
	4	10½"	#5, 11, 13, 14
	1	8½"	#10
	3	4½"	#4, 7, 16
	7	2½"	"c",
Red	2	12½"	#6, 15
	1	8½"	#9
	2	6½"	#3, #12
Leg Unit	1	2½" x 10½"	#8

BLOCK E ASSEMBLY:

Snowball Corners:

 You need #3, 6, 9 & 15 and 7 White squares.

 Refer to the Snowball Corners diagram.

 Carefully note the direction of each diagonal.

#3, 6 & 15: Align a White square with both ends.

#9: Align a White square with 1 end.

 Draw the diagonals and sew on the line.

 Fold back the flap and press.

Assembly: Arrange the pieces on a work surface or table.

 Column 1: #1

 Column 2: Sew 2-3-4. Press.

 Column 3: Sew 5-6-7. Press.

 Column 4: Sew 8-9-10. Press.

 Column 5: Sew 11-12-13. Press.

 Column 6: Sew 14-15-16. Press.

 Column 7: #17

Sew the columns together. Press.

Sew Sash O to the bottom of the piece. Press.

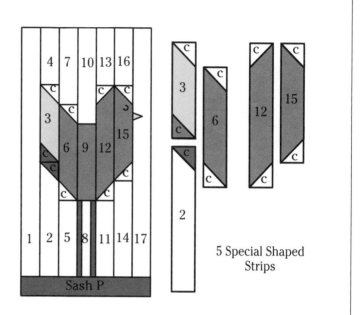

5 Special Shaped
Strips

BLOCK F:

CUTTING CHART

Color	Quantity	Length	Position
White yardage	2	26½"	#1, 17
	1	12½"	#2
	2	10½"	#10, 14
	3	8½"	#5, 7, 11
	3	6½"	#4, 13, 16
	7	2½"	"c"
Red	2	2½"	#2c, 3c
Gold	1	12½"	#12
	3	10½"	#3, 6, 15
	1	8½"	#9
Leg Unit	1	2½" x 8½"	#8

BLOCK F ASSEMBLY:

Follow the instructions for Block B.

Sew Sash P to the bottom of the piece. Press.

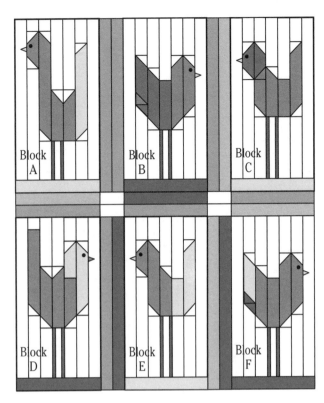

Roosters - Quilt Assembly Diagram

ASSEMBLY:
Arrange all blocks on a work surface or table.
Refer to diagram for block placement and direction.

Row 1:
Sew Block A - J & K - Block B - L & M - Block C. Press.

Row 2:
Sew Block D - Q & R - Block E - S & T - Block F. Press.
Sew the rows together. Press.

BORDERS:
Pieced Border #1:
Sew varied lengths (12" to 24") of Turquoise and Green end to
end to make a piece 124" long. Press.
Cut 2 pieces 60½" long.
Sew a strip to the left and right side of the quilt. Press.

Pieced Border #2:
Sew varied lengths (12" to 24") of Turquoise and Green end to
end to make a piece 240" long. Press.
Cut 2 strips 2½" x 60½" for sides.
Cut 2 strips 2½" x 58½" for top and bottom.
Sew side borders to the quilt. Press.
Sew top and bottom borders to the quilt. Press.

Outer Border #3:
Cut strips 4½" wide parallel to the selvage to eliminate piecing.
Cut 2 strips 4½" x 64½" for sides.
Cut 2 strips 4½" x 66½" for top and bottom.
Sew side borders to the quilt. Press.
Sew top and bottom borders to the quilt. Press.

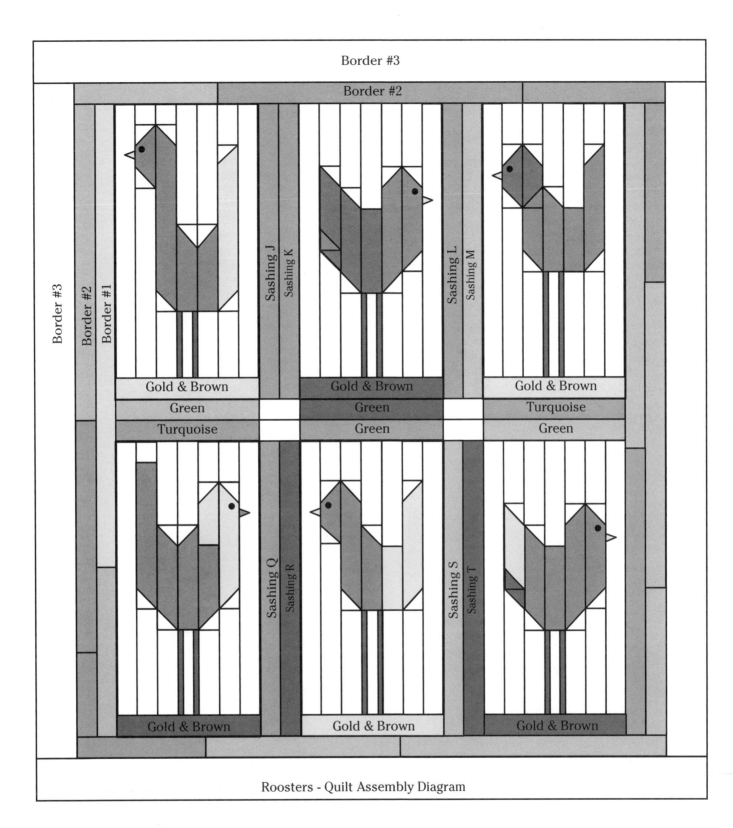

Roosters - Quilt Assembly Diagram

FINISHING:

Applique:

See Basic Instructions.

For each beak, fold a 1½" square of fabric into a beak shape. Applique as desired.

Quilting:

See Basic Instructions.

Binding:

Cut strips 2½" wide.

Sew together end to end to equal 286".

See Binding Instructions.

Sew buttons in place for eyes.

Note: This quilt is also available as a pattern pack #0951 "Roosters in the Morning" by Design Originals.

Scroll Birds

photo is on page 5

SIZE: 39½" x 44"
TIP: Add more borders to make a larger quilt.

YARDAGE:
Yardage is given for using either fabric yardage or
    'Layer Cake' squares.
We used a *Moda* "Nest" by Tula Pink
    'Layer Cake' collection of 10" x 10" fabric squares
    - we purchased 1 'Layer Cake' and used the leftovers
    from the Bluebirds Quilt on page 6.

8 squares	OR	⅝ yard Red
5 squares	OR	⅝ yard Gold

Center, Geese & Corners	Purchase 1¼ yard Brown
Border #2 & Binding	Purchase 1⅓ yard Red
Backing	Purchase 1⅞ yards
Batting	Purchase 48" x 52"

Sewing machine, needle, thread
DMC pearl cotton or 6-ply floss
#22 or #24 chenille needle
5 Black ⅜" buttons

PREPARATION FOR SQUARES:
    Cut all squares 10" x 10".
    Label the stacks or pieces as you cut.

SORTING:
    Sort the following 10" x 10" squares into stacks:

POSITION	QUANTITY & COLOR
Flying Geese	3 Gold, 4 Red
Corner Squares	2 Red
Applique	1 Red, 1 Gold

CENTER:
Cut 1 rectangle 14" x 18½" from Brown yardage.

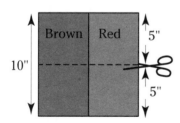

Corner Block
Cutting Diagram
Make 4

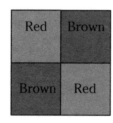

Corner Block
Assembly Diagram
Make 4

CORNER BLOCKS:
    Cut 4 Red and 4 Brown rectangles 5" x 10".
    Refer to the Corner Block Cutting Diagram.
    Sew a Red and Brown rectangle together to make a
        unit 9½" x 10".

    Cut the strip into 2 units 5" x 9½".
    Refer to the Corner Block Assembly Diagram.
    Sew the 2 units together. Press.
    Make 4.

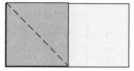

Align a square with the end of the strip. Draw a diagonal line and sew on the line. Fold back the triangle.

Repeat on the other end of the strip. Press.

Flying Geese Diagram

FLYING GEESE BLOCKS:
    Cut 8 Red and 6 Gold rectangles 5" x 9½".
    Cut 28 squares 5" x 5" from Brown yardage.
    Refer to the Flying Geese Diagram.
    Make 14 Flying Geese.

Preparation of Flying Geese Border #1:
Left Side:
Sew 3 Red geese together with the points down.
    Press.

Right Side:
Sew geese with the points up Red-Gold-Red.
    Press.

Top:
Sew geese with the points facing left:
    Red-Gold-Red-Gold. Press.

Bottom:
Sew geese with the points facing right:
    Gold-Gold-Gold-Red. Press.

Scroll Birds
Quilt Assembly Diagram

ASSEMBLY AND BORDERS:
 Arrange all blocks on a work surface or table.
 Refer to diagram for block placement and direction.

Flying Geese Border #1:
 Sew a Corner square to each end of the top and bottom
  Flying Geese borders. Press.
 Sew side borders to the quilt. Press.
 Sew top and bottom borders to the quilt. Press.

Border #2:
Cut strips 4½" wide parallel to the selvage to eliminate piecing.
 Cut 2 strips 4½" x 32" for sides.
 Cut 2 strips 4½" x 44½" for top and bottom.
 Sew side borders to the quilt. Press.
 Sew top and bottom borders to the quilt. Press.

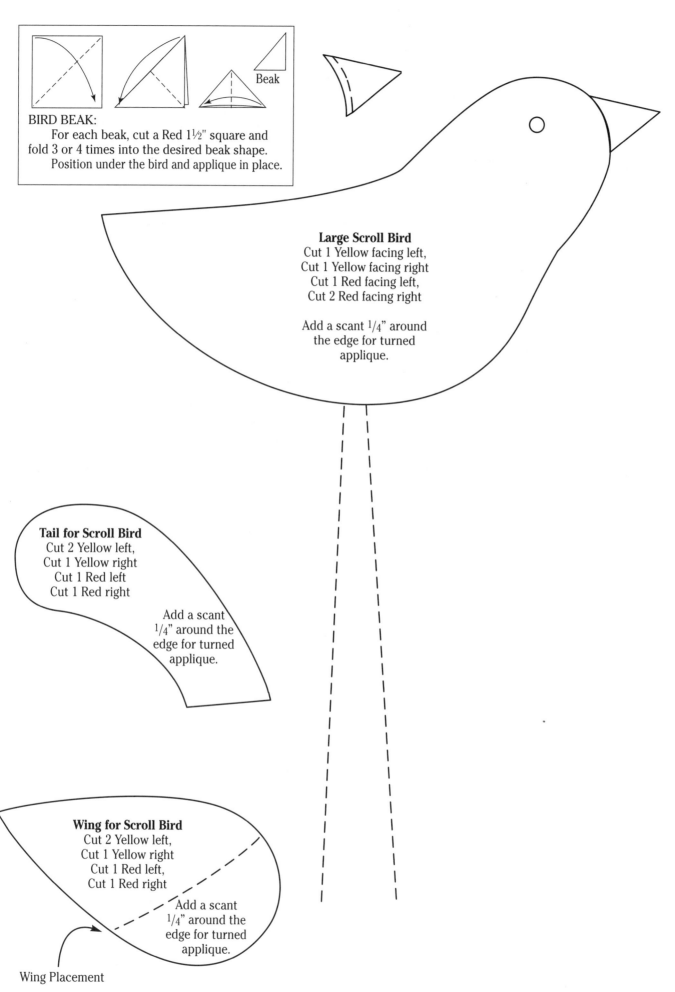

BIRD BEAK:
   For each beak, cut a Red 1½" square and
fold 3 or 4 times into the desired beak shape.
   Position under the bird and applique in place.

Beak

Large Scroll Bird
Cut 1 Yellow facing left,
Cut 1 Yellow facing right
Cut 1 Red facing left,
Cut 2 Red facing right

Add a scant ¼" around
the edge for turned
applique.

Tail for Scroll Bird
Cut 2 Yellow left,
Cut 1 Yellow right
Cut 1 Red left
Cut 1 Red right

Add a scant
¼" around the
edge for turned
applique.

Wing for Scroll Bird
Cut 2 Yellow left,
Cut 1 Yellow right
Cut 1 Red left,
Cut 1 Red right

Add a scant
¼" around the
edge for turned
applique.

Wing Placement

Scroll Birds
Applique Placement Diagram

Bird Pattern
Placement
Diagram

APPLIQUE:
See Basic Instructions.
    Cut pieces using patterns. Applique as desired.
    Beaks: Cut a 1½" square for each beak and fold into
        a beak shape.
    Position under the body and applique as desired.
    Embroider legs with a Running stitch.
    Sew buttons in place for eyes.

FINISHING:
Quilting: See Basic Instructions.
Binding: Cut strips 2½" wide.
        Sew together end to end to equal 178".
        See Binding Instructions.

Bluebirds Quilt

photo is on pages 6 - 7

SIZE: 60" x 71½"

YARDAGE:

Yardage is given for using either fabric yardage or
'Layer Cake' squares.

We used a *Moda* "Nest" by Tula Pink
'Layer Cake' collection of 10" x 10" fabric squares
- we purchased 1 'Layer Cake'

9 squares	OR	⅞ yard Green
9 squares	OR	⅞ yard Turquoise
4 squares	OR	⅓ yard White

Applique bird beaks	5" x 5" scrap of Bright Yellow
Sashing	Purchase 1 yard White
Border #1	Purchase ½ yard Turquoise
Border #2 & binding	Purchase 2 yards Turquoise print
Backing	Purchase 3½ yards
Batting	Purchase 68" x 80"

Sewing machine, needle, thread
DMC pearl cotton or 6-ply floss
#22 or #24 chenille needle

PREPARATION FOR BLOCKS:

Cut all squares 10" x 10".
Label the stacks or pieces as you cut.

SORTING:

Sort the following 10" x 10" squares into stacks:

POSITION	QUANTITY & COLOR	
2, 3, 5, 9, 11, 13, 16, 18, 19	9	Green
1, 7, 14, 20	4	White
4, 6, 8, 10, 12, 15, 17	7	Turquoise
Applique Birds 1, 7, 14, 20	2	Turquoise

CUTTING:

Cut 20 White Sash A - 2½" x 10"
Cut 20 White Sash B - 2½" x 12"
Cut 1 White bottom Sash C - 2½" x 46½"
Cut 1 White side Sash D - 2½" x 60"

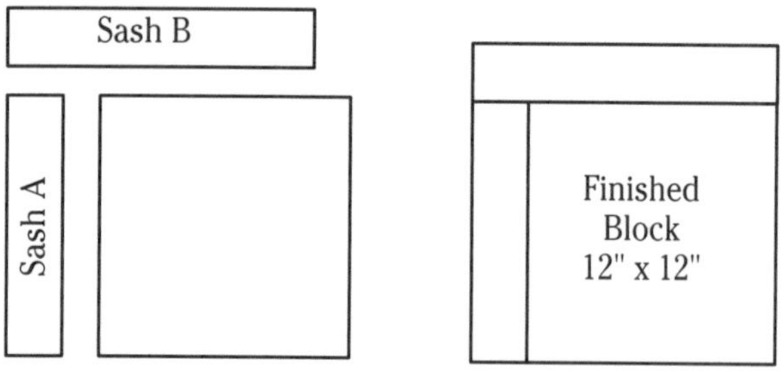

Sash B

Sash A

Finished
Block
12" x 12"

SEW BLOCKS:

Refer to the Block diagram.

For each block, sew a Sash A to the left side of the
block. Press.

For each block, sew a Sash B to the top of the
block. Press.

Each block will measure 12" x 12" at this point.

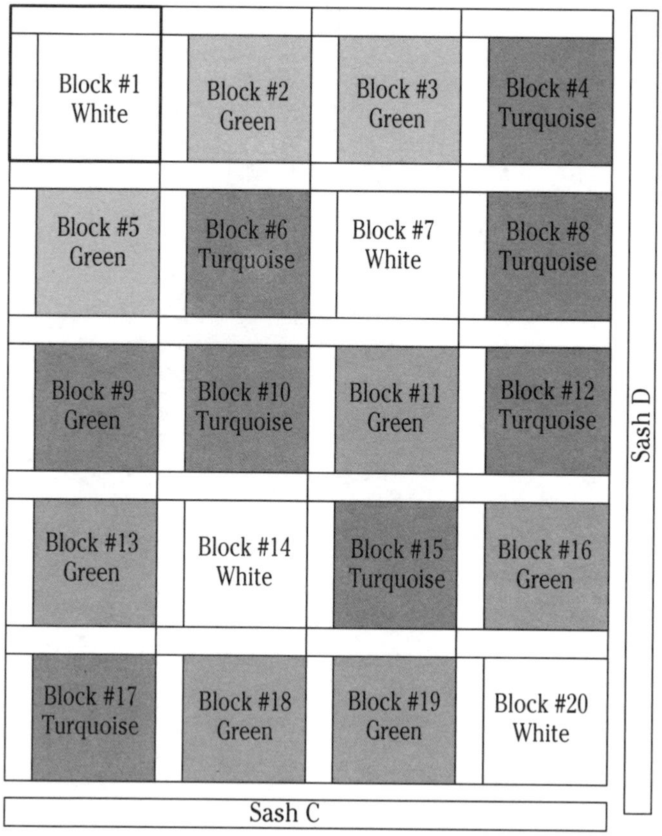

Block #1 White	Block #2 Green	Block #3 Green	Block #4 Turquoise	
Block #5 Green	Block #6 Turquoise	Block #7 White	Block #8 Turquoise	
Block #9 Green	Block #10 Turquoise	Block #11 Green	Block #12 Turquoise	Sash D
Block #13 Green	Block #14 White	Block #15 Turquoise	Block #16 Green	
Block #17 Turquoise	Block #18 Green	Block #19 Green	Block #20 White	

Sash C

ASSEMBLY:

Arrange all blocks on a work surface or table.
Refer to diagram for block placement and direction.
Sew blocks together in 5 rows, 4 blocks per row. Press.

Sew rows together. Press.

Sew bottom Sash C to the quilt. Press.
Sew side Sash D to the quilt. Press.

Bluebirds - Quilt Assembly Diagram

APPLIQUE:
Cut out applique pieces from patterns.
See Applique Instructions.
Embroider bird eyes and legs with a Running stitch.

Inner Border #1:
Cut strips 2½" by the width of fabric.
Sew strips together end to end.
Cut 2 strips 2½" x 60" for sides.
Cut 2 strips 2½" x 52½" for top and bottom.
Sew side borders to the quilt. Press.
Sew top and bottom borders to the quilt. Press.

Outer Border #2:
Cut strips 4½" wide parallel to the selvage to
eliminate piecing.
Cut 2 strips 4½" x 64" for sides.
Cut 2 strips 4½" x 60½" for top and bottom.
Sew side borders to the quilt. Press.
Sew top and bottom borders to the quilt. Press.

FINISHING:
Quilting: See Basic Instructions
Binding: Cut strips 2½" wide.
Sew together end to end to equal 273".
See Binding Instructions.

Bird wing placement on Bird back

Wings for Right Bluebird
Cut 1 Turquoise
Cut 1 Dark Turquoise

Add a scant 1/4" around the edge for turned applique.

Tail for Right Bluebird
Cut 1 Turquoise
Cut 1 Dark Turquoise

Add a scant 1/4" around the edge for turned applique.

Right Bluebird
Cut 1 Turquoise
Cut 1 Dark Turquoise

Add a scant 1/4" around the edge for turned applique

Bird Pattern Placement Diagram

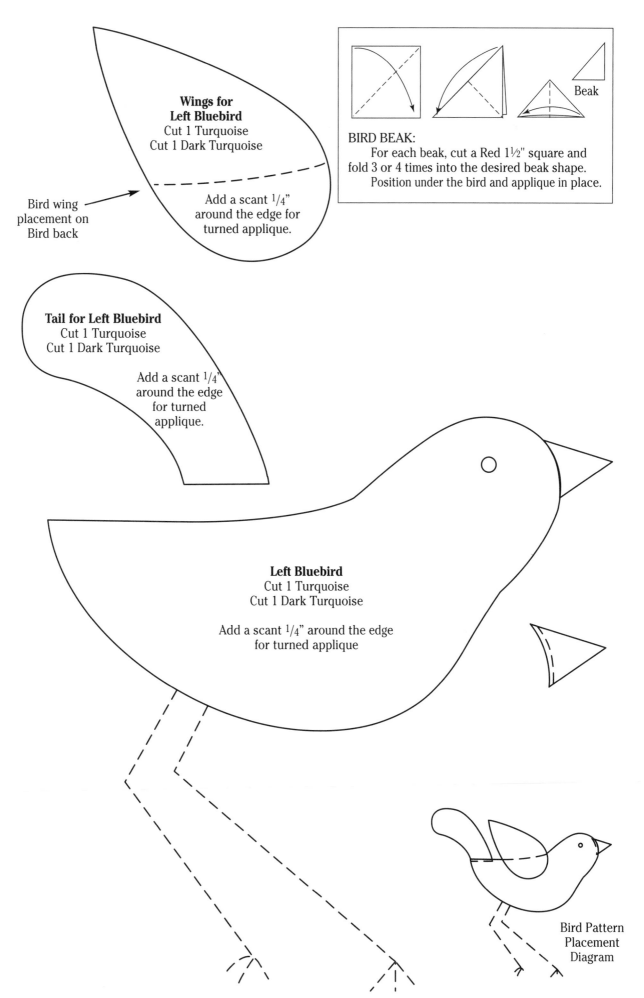

**Wings for
Left Bluebird**
Cut 1 Turquoise
Cut 1 Dark Turquoise

Bird wing
placement on
Bird back

Add a scant ¹/₄"
around the edge for
turned applique.

BIRD BEAK:
    For each beak, cut a Red 1¹/₂" square and
fold 3 or 4 times into the desired beak shape.
Position under the bird and applique in place.

Beak

Tail for Left Bluebird
Cut 1 Turquoise
Cut 1 Dark Turquoise

Add a scant ¹/₄'
around the edge
for turned
applique.

Left Bluebird
Cut 1 Turquoise
Cut 1 Dark Turquoise

Add a scant ¹/₄" around the edge
for turned applique

Bird Pattern
Placement
Diagram

Bluebird Pillow

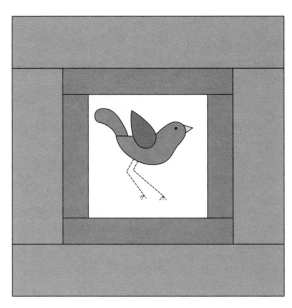
Appliqued Bluebird Pillow

photo is on page 6
SIZE: 21½" x 21½"

YARDAGE:
Yardage is given for using either fabric yardage or
    'Layer Cake' squares.
We used a *Moda* "Nest" by Tula Pink
    'Layer Cake' collection of 10" x 10" fabric squares
    - we used 3 squares leftover from the Bluebirds Quilt

1 square	OR	⅓ yard White
1 square	OR	⅓ yard Light Turquoise
1 square	OR	⅓ yard Dark Turquoise

Applique bird beak	2" scrap of Bright Yellow
Border #1	Purchase ⅙ yard Dark Turquoise
Border #2 & Backing	Purchase 1 yard Light Turquoise
Batting	Purchase 21½" x 21½"

14" pillow form
Sewing machine, needle, thread
DMC pearl cotton or 6-ply floss
#22 or #24 chenille needle

SORTING:
    Sort the following 10" x 10" squares into stacks:

POSITION	QUANTITY & COLOR	
Center	1	White
Appliques	2	Turquoise

CUTTING:
    Cut White Center block 10" x 10".
    For Pillow Back, cut the following Turquoise pieces:
    16½" x 22"
    13½" x 22"

BORDERS:
Border #1:
    Cut 2 strips 2½" x 10" for sides.
    Cut 2 strips 2½" x 14" for top and bottom.
    Sew side borders to the block. Press.
    Sew top and bottom borders to the block. Press.

Border #2:
    Cut 2 strips 4½" x 14" for sides.
    Cut 2 strips 4½" x 22" for top and bottom.
    Sew side borders to the block. Press.
    Sew top and bottom borders to the block. Press.

APPLIQUE:
    Use the Patterns for the Bluebird.
    Applique bird, beak and wing.
    Embroider the legs with a Running stitch.

QUILTING:
    Refer to the Basic Instructions.
    Align the batting with the top layer.
    Quilt the center and first border areas only.

PILLOW BACK:
    Press and sew a 1" hem along one 22" edge of
        each Turquoise piece.
    With right sides together, align the pillow back
        pieces with the edge of the pillow front. The
        hemmed edges will overlap near the center
        of the pillow.
    Sew a ¼" seam all around the pillow.
    Turn the pillow right side out.

FINISHING:
Quilting:
Stitch in the ditch along the outer edge of Border 1.
Quilt the outer border as desired.

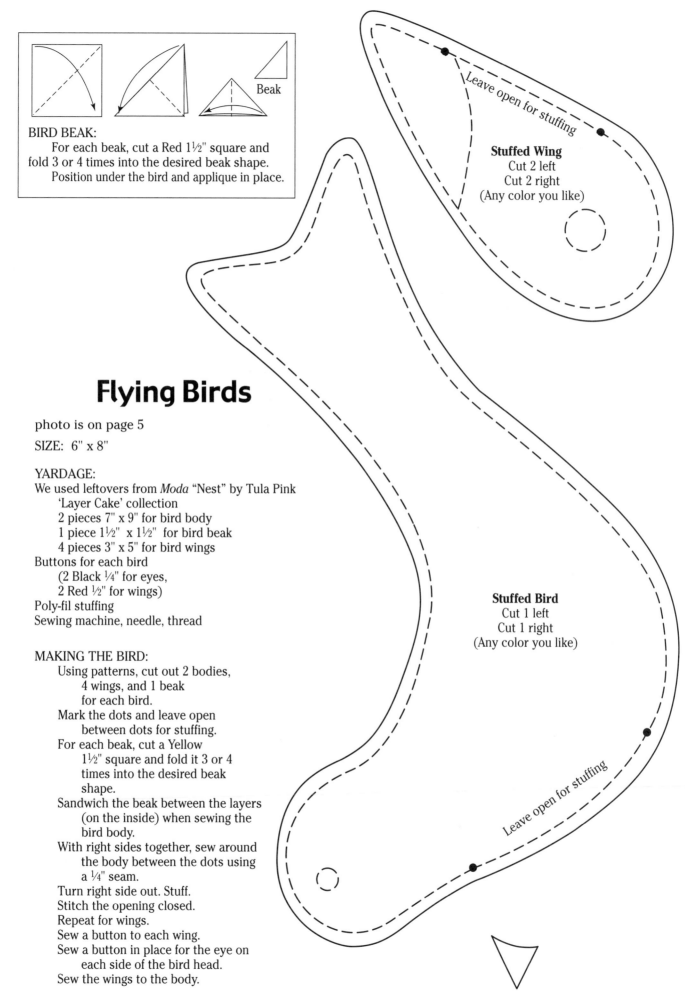

BIRD BEAK:
    For each beak, cut a Red 1½" square and fold 3 or 4 times into the desired beak shape. Position under the bird and applique in place.

Beak

Leave open for stuffing

Stuffed Wing
Cut 2 left
Cut 2 right
(Any color you like)

Flying Birds

photo is on page 5

SIZE: 6" x 8"

YARDAGE:
We used leftovers from *Moda* "Nest" by Tula Pink
    'Layer Cake' collection
    2 pieces 7" x 9" for bird body
    1 piece 1½" x 1½" for bird beak
    4 pieces 3" x 5" for bird wings
Buttons for each bird
    (2 Black ¼" for eyes,
    2 Red ½" for wings)
Poly-fil stuffing
Sewing machine, needle, thread

MAKING THE BIRD:
    Using patterns, cut out 2 bodies,
        4 wings, and 1 beak
        for each bird.
    Mark the dots and leave open
        between dots for stuffing.
    For each beak, cut a Yellow
        1½" square and fold it 3 or 4
        times into the desired beak
        shape.
    Sandwich the beak between the layers
        (on the inside) when sewing the
        bird body.
    With right sides together, sew around
        the body between the dots using
        a ¼" seam.
    Turn right side out. Stuff.
    Stitch the opening closed.
    Repeat for wings.
    Sew a button to each wing.
    Sew a button in place for the eye on
        each side of the bird head.
    Sew the wings to the body.

Stuffed Bird
Cut 1 left
Cut 1 right
(Any color you like)

Leave open for stuffing

Round & Round

photo is on pages 8 - 9

SIZE: 48" x 57"
TIP: Add more borders to make a larger quilt.

YARDAGE:
Yardage is given for using either fabric yardage or
    'Layer Cake' squares.
We used a *Moda* "Bistro" by Deb Strain
    'Layer Cake' collection of 10" x 10" fabric squares
    - we purchased 1 'Layer Cake'

9 squares	OR	⅞ yard Turquoise
7 squares	OR	⅝ yard Black
5 squares	OR	⅝ yard Brown
4 squares	OR	⅓ yard Red
4 squares	OR	⅓ yard Lime Green
4 squares	OR	⅓ yard Dark Brown
4 squares	OR	⅓ yard Tan

Border #1 & Sashings	Purchase ½ yard Dark Brown
Border #2 & Binding	Purchase 1½ yards Dark Red
Backing	Purchase 2⅝ yards
Batting	Purchase 56" x 65"

Sewing machine, needle, thread

For Applique:
    1 no-melt plastic template & spray starch
        (or 1½ yards of Wash-Away Tear-Away stabilizer
        and a glue stick)
    Optional: June Tailor Simple Circles templates to
        make cutting easier.

PREPARATION FOR SQUARES:
    Cut all squares 10" x 10".
    Label the stacks or pieces as you cut.

SORTING:
    Sort the following 10" x 10" squares into stacks:

POSITION	QUANTITY & COLOR	
Semicircles	9	Turquoise
Semicircle background	6	Black
	3	Tan
Quarter circles	4	Lime Green
Quarter circle background	4	Dark Brown
Cornerstones	1	Black
	1	Tan
	1	Brown
Flying Geese background	4	Brown
Flying Geese squares	4	Red

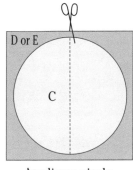

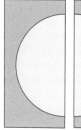

Applique circle
to background.

Cut entire
piece in half.

Turquoise Half-Circles Diagram

Cut Pieces for Turquoise Circle Blocks:

TIP: Use the template patterns on page 5 (or use a
June Tailor Simple Circles template to make cutting easier).

Circle C	Cut 9	Turquoise	7½" x 7½"
Template C	Cut 1	Plastic (or 9 Stabilizer)	7" x 7"
Square D	Cut 6	Black squares	9½" x 10"
Square E	Cut 3	Tan squares	9½" x 10"

Applique the Turquoise Circles:

See Basic Applique instructions.

Applique a circle in the center of each Black square.
Applique a circle in the center of each Tan square.
Tip: Work gently to avoid stretching the bias edge of the circle.

Cut each circle-background to make 2 pieces 5" x 9½".
Make 12 with a Black background.
Make 6 with a Tan background.

Sew 3 Half-Circles with Tan backgrounds end to end
to make a piece 5" x 27½".
Press. Make 2.

Sew 3 Half-Circles with Black backgrounds end to end
to make a piece 5" x 27½".
Press. Make 4.

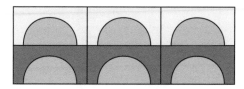

Tan & Black Borders - Make 2

Sew a unit of Half-Circles with Black background
to a unit of Half-Circles with Tan background.
This will be the Top Border.

Repeat to make the Bottom Border.
Each unit will measure 9½" x 27½".
Press.

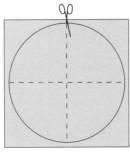 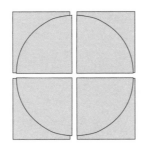

Stack 4 squares and cut in half twice to make 4 pieces.

Mix up the fabrics and resew.

Lime Pieced Squares Diagram

Make Pieced Lime Squares:

Stack 4 squares and cut them in half twice to make 4 pieces. Mix up the fabrics so each square has 4 different fabrics. Resew them into squares.

Press. Make 4.

Cut pieces for Lime Circle Blocks:

TIP: Use the template patterns on page 5 (or use a *June Tailor* Simple Circles template to make cutting easier).

Circle F	Cut 4	Lime	8½" x 8½"
Template F	Cut 1	Plastic (or 4 Stabilizer)	8" x 8"
Square G	Cut 4	Dark Brown squares	9½" x 9½"

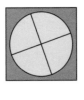　

Applique the Lime Circles:

See Basic Applique instructions.

Applique a Lime circle in the center of each Dark Brown 9½" x 9½" square. Press. Make 4.

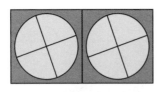

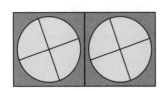

Sew 2 Dark Brown squares in a row.

Sew 2 rows. Each row will measure 9½" x 18½". Press.

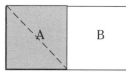 

Align a square with the end of the block. Sew a diagonal line as shown. Fold back the triangle. Press.

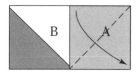 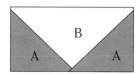

Align a square with the other end of the block. Sew a diagonal line as shown. Fold back the triangle. Press.

Flying Geese Diagrams

FLYING GEESE UNITS:

Make Star Points Units

Square A	Cut 16 Red squares	5" x 5"
Rectangle B	Cut 8 Brown strips	5" x 9½"

Refer to the Flying Geese Diagram above to make Star Points units. Press. Make 8.

Star Points unit
Make 8

CUT CORNERS:

Cut the following corners from Brown:
Corners M   4 squares   5" x 5"

ASSEMBLY:

Star Center:

Arrange all blocks on a work surface or table.
Refer to the Center Assembly diagram for block placement.

Top - Star Points Border:

Sew M - Star Points unit - Star Points unit - M together.
Press. Make 2.

Center - Star Points and Brown Squares:

Sew Star Points unit - 2 Brown Squares - Star Points unit.
Press. Make 2.

Sew the Quilt Center:

Sew all 4 rows together. Press.

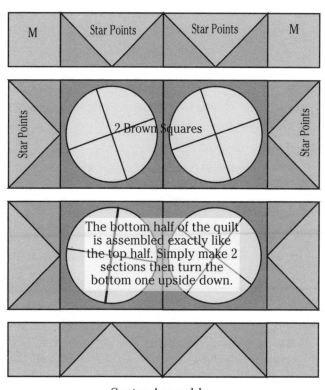

Center Assembly

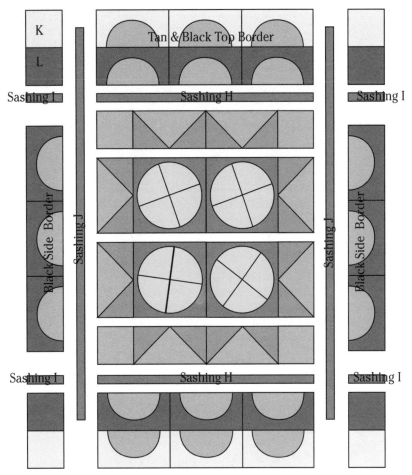

Tan & Black Bottom Border

CUT SASHING STRIPS:

Cut the following Sashing strips from Dark Brown:

Top and Bottom Sashing H	2 strips	1½" x 27½"
Top & Bottom Side Sashing I	4 strips	1½" x 5½"
Long Side Sashing J	2 strips	1½" x 47½"

CUT CORNER SQUARES:

Corner square K	4 Tan	5" x 5"
Corner square L	4 Black	5" x 5"

Sew corner squares K and L together to make a unit 5" x 9½".
Make 4. Press.

ASSEMBLY:

Arrange all blocks and sashing on a work surface or table.
Refer to the Quilt Assembly diagram for block placement.

Star Center:

Sew a 27½" Sashing H to the top and bottom of the
Center unit. Press.
Sew the Top and Bottom Tan & Black Borders to the
Center. Press.
Sew a 47½" Sashing J to the right and left sides of the
Center. Press.

Side Strips:

Sew the following into borders for the side:
K/L corner - Sashing I - Black Side Border - Sashing I - K/L
corner.
Press. Make 2.

Sew a Side strip to the right and left sides of the quilt.
Press.

Round & Round - Assembly Diagram

Border #1:
Cut strips 1½" by the width of fabric.
Sew strips together end to end.
> Cut 2 strips 1½" x 47½" for sides.
> Cut 2 strips 1½" x 40½" for top and bottom.
> Sew side borders to the quilt. Press.
> Sew top and bottom borders to the quilt. Press.

Border #2:
Cut strips 4½" wide parallel to the selvage to eliminate piecing.
> Cut 2 strips 4½" x 49½" for sides.
> Cut 2 strips 4½" x 48½" for top and bottom.
> Sew side borders to the quilt. Press.
> Sew top and bottom borders to the quilt. Press.

FINISHING:

Quilting: See Basic Instructions.

Binding: Cut strips 2½" wide.
> Sew together end to end to equal 220".
> See Binding Instructions.

Note: This quilt is also available as a pattern pack
#0956 "Round & Round" by Design Originals.

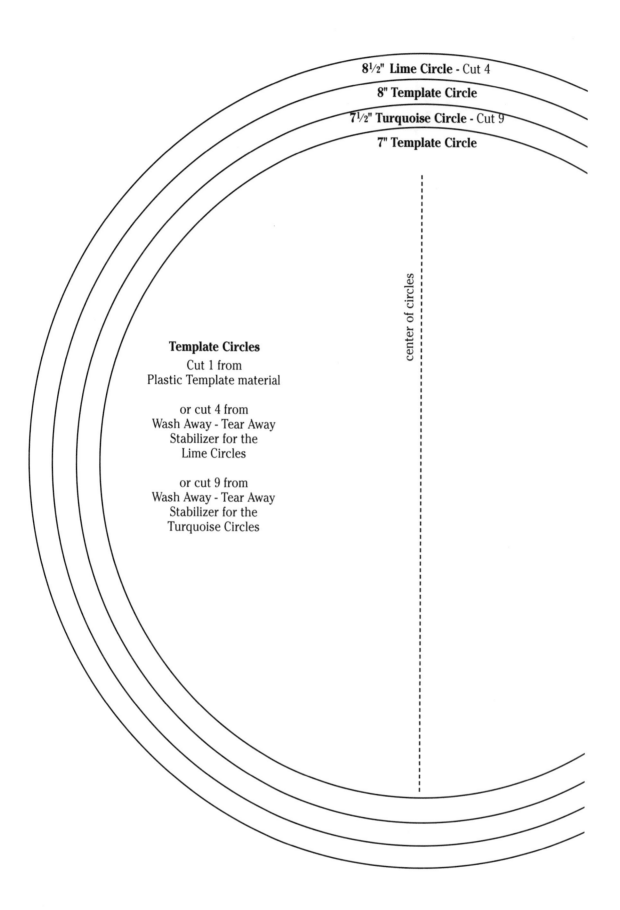

8¹/₂" Lime Circle - Cut 4

8" Template Circle

7¹/₂" Turquoise Circle - Cut 9

7" Template Circle

center of circles

Template Circles
Cut 1 from
Plastic Template material

or cut 4 from
Wash Away - Tear Away
Stabilizer for the
Lime Circles

or cut 9 from
Wash Away - Tear Away
Stabilizer for the
Turquoise Circles

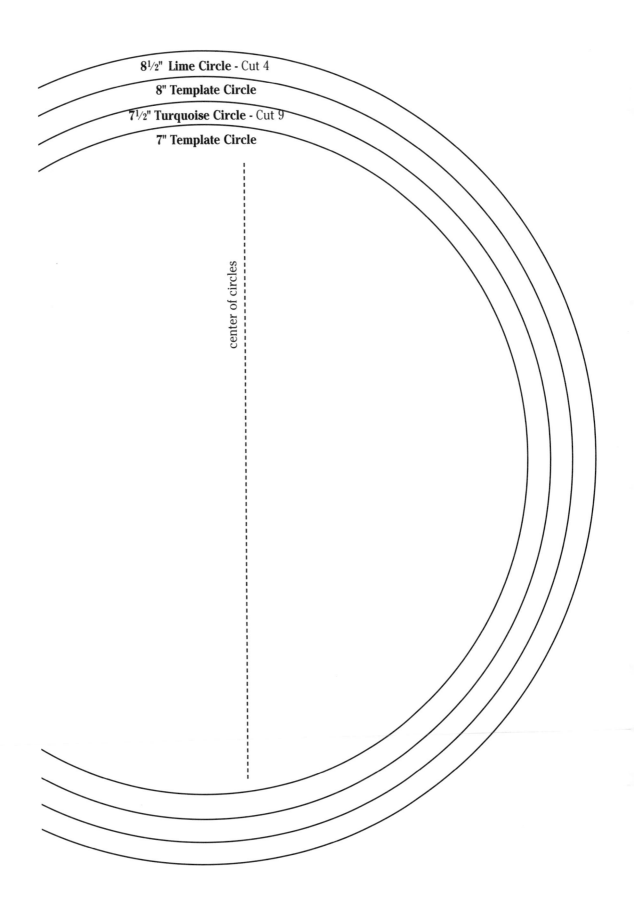

8½" **Lime Circle** - Cut 4

8" **Template Circle**

7½" **Turquoise Circle** - Cut 9

7" **Template Circle**

center of circles

Striped Pinwheels

photo is on pages 10 - 11

SIZE: 64" x 84"

YARDAGE:

Yardage is given for using either fabric yardage or
   'Jelly Roll' strips.
We used a *Moda* "Cotton Blossoms" by Bonnie of Cotton Way
   and Camille of Thimble Blossoms
   'Jelly Roll' collection of 2½" fabric strips
   - we purchased 1 'Jelly Roll'

8 strips	OR	⅝ yard Tan
8 strips	OR	⅝ yard Red
8 strips	OR	⅝ yard Dark Brown
4 strips	OR	⅓ yard Medium Brown
4 strips	OR	⅓ yard Green
2 strips	OR	⅙ yard Green plaid
2 strips	OR	⅙ yard Green stripe
2 strips	OR	⅙ yard Red plaid
2 strips	OR	⅙ yard Red stripe

Border #2   Purchase ½ yard Medium Brown
Border #3, Corner squares & Binding   Purchase 2⅛ yards Red
Backing   Purchase 5⅛ yards
Batting   Purchase 72" x 92"
Sewing machine, needle, thread

PREPARATION FOR STRIPS:
   Cut all strips 2½" by the width of fabric
     (usually 42" - 44").
   Label the stacks or pieces as you cut.

SORTING:
   Sort the following 2½" strips into stacks:

POSITION	QUANTITY & COLOR
Block 1:	4 Medium Brown, 1 Green stripe
Blocks 2 & 5:	8 Dark Brown, 1 Green stripe, 1 Red stripe
Blocks 3 & 6:	8 Red, 2 Red plaid
Block 4:	4 Green, 1 Red stripe
Border #1:	8 Tan, 2 Green plaid

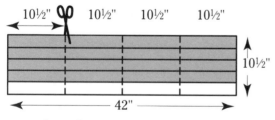

Strip Construction Diagram

BLOCK ASSEMBLY:
Block 1:
   Cut 1 Green stripe and 4 Medium Brown strips 2½" x 42".
   Refer to the Strip Construction diagram.
   Sew 1 Stripe and 4 Brown strips together to make a
     piece 10½" x 42".
   Cut the piece into 4 squares 10½" x 10½".

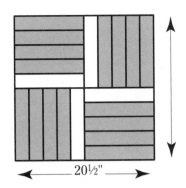

Block Assembly Diagram

Refer to the Block Assembly Diagram.
Arrange the squares as shown.
Sew the squares together in 2 rows of 2 squares
    per row.
Sew the rows together. Press.
Repeat for remaining blocks.

Block 2 uses 1 Green stripe and 4 Dark Brown strips.
Blocks 3 and 6 use 1 Red plaid and 4 Red strips each.
Block 4 uses 1 Red stripe and 4 Green strips.
Block 5 uses 1 Red stripe and 4 Dark Brown strips.
    Each block will measure 20½" x 20½" at this point.

    Refer to diagram for block placement and direction.
    Sew blocks together in 3 rows, 2 blocks per row. Press.
    Sew rows together. Press

QUILT ASSEMBLY:
    Arrange all blocks on a work surface or table.

BORDERS:
Pieced Border #1:
Pieced Side strips: You need 6 Tan strips.
    Sew Tan strips end to end. Press.
    Cut 4 strips 2½" x 60½".
    Sew the strips together in pairs to make a piece
        4½" x 60½" for each side.
    Sew a strip set to each side of the quilt. Press.
Pieced Corners: From the Red fabric for Border #3,
        cut 2 strips 2½" x 18".
    Sew the strips together to make a piece 4½" x 18".
    Cut the piece into 4 squares 4½" x 4½".

Pieced Top & Bottom Strips:
You need 2 Tan and 2 Green plaid strips.
    Sew a Tan and Plaid together to make a piece 4½" x 40½".
    Make 2.
    Sew a Red corner square to each end of both strips.
    Sew a strip to the top and bottom of the quilt. Press.

Inner Border #2:
Cut strips 2½" by the width of fabric.
Sew strips together end to end.
    Cut 2 strips 2½" x 68½" for sides.
    Cut 2 strips 2½" x 52½" for top and bottom.
    Sew side borders to the quilt. Press.
    Sew top and bottom borders to the quilt. Press.

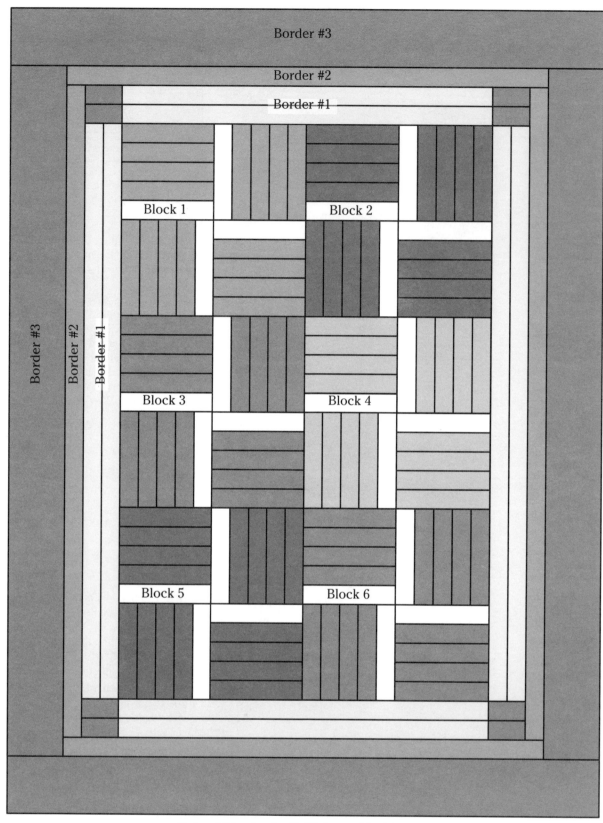

Striped Pinwheel - Quilt Assembly Diagram

Outer Border #3:
Cut strips 6½" wide parallel to the selvage to eliminate piecing.

    Cut 2 strips 6½" x 72½" for sides.
    Cut 2 strips 6½" x 64½" for top and bottom.
    Sew side borders to the quilt. Press.
    Sew top and bottom borders to the quilt. Press.

FINISHING:
Quilting: See Basic Instructions.
Binding: Cut strips 2½" wide.
    Sew together end to end to equal 306".
    See Binding Instructions

Rainbow of Colors

photo is on page 12

SIZE: 86" x 100"
TIP: Add more borders to make a larger quilt.

YARDAGE:
Yardage is given for using either fabric yardage or 'Jelly Roll' strips.
We used a *Moda* "Butterfly Fling" by Me & My Sister
'Jelly Roll' collection of 2½" fabric strips
- we purchased 2 'Jelly Rolls'

15 strips	OR	1⅛ yard Green
14 strips	OR	1⅛ yard Aqua
15 strips	OR	1⅛ yard Purple
15 strips	OR	1⅛ yard Pink
10 strips	OR	¾ yard Yellow
6 strips	OR	½ yard White with Yellow and Aqua prints

Border #1	Purchase ½ yard Aqua
Border #2	Purchase ½ yard Purple
Border #3 & Binding	Purchase 2½ yards White
Backing	Purchase 7⅙ yards
Batting	Purchase 94" x 108"

Sewing machine, needle, thread

PREPARATION FOR STRIPS:
Cut all strips 2½" by the width of fabric (usually 42" - 44").
Label the stacks or pieces as you cut.

SORTING:
Sort the following 2½" strips into stacks.

POSITION	QUANTITY & COLOR
Blocks #1, 5, 9, 10, 13, 14, 17, 18, 21, 22, 26, 30	15 Green
Blocks #1, 2, 6, 10, 14, 15, 18, 19, 22, 23, 26, 27	14 Aqua and 1 White with Aqua print
Blocks #2, 3, 6, 7, 11, 15, 19, 20, 23, 24, 27, 28	15 Lavender
Blocks #3, 4, 7, 8, 11, 12, 16, 20, 24, 25, 28, 29	15 Pink
Blocks #4, 5, 8, 9, 12, 13, 16, 17, 21, 25, 29, 30	10 Yellow and 5 White with Yellow print

TIP: We fussy cut the smaller areas of White with Yellow print and
White with Aqua print and sorted them into the stacks.

CUTTING:
From the fabric for Border #2
Cut 30 Lavender Center squares (C) 2½" x 2½".

CUT STRIPS:
Cut the indicated lengths of strips:
Refer to the Log Cabin Placement diagram.
TIP: To avoid confusion, number the cut pieces.

TIP FOR SORTING:
We added White strips with Aqua print into the
   Aqua stack.
We added White strips with Yellow print into the
   Yellow stack.

TIP: Cut the longest strips first.

**Preparation for
Green-Aqua Blocks 1, 10, 14, 18, 22, & 26:**
From Green print strips, cut 6 each of the following:
   #1: 2½" x 2½"
   #2: 2½" x 4½"
   #5: 2½" x 6½"
   #6: 2½" x 8½"
   #9: 2½" x 10½"
   #10: 2½" x 12½"
(You will have 6 of each number.)

From Aqua print strips, cut 6 each of the following:
   #3: 2½" x 4½"
   #4: 2½" x 6½"
   #7: 2½" x 8½"
   #8: 2½" x 10½"
   #11: 2½" x 12½"
   #12: 2½" x 14½"
(You will have 6 of each number.)

This gives you all the pieces needed.
   Make all 6 Green-Aqua blocks.

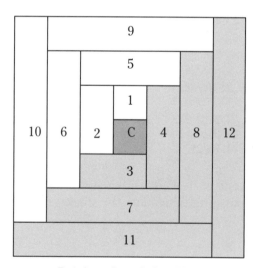

Rainbow Log Cabin Block

SEW BLOCKS:
Piece all 6 Green-Aqua blocks in the following sequence:
   Sew the Center square to #1. Press.
   Sew   C-1 to   #2.   Press.
   Sew   C-1-2 to   #3.   Press.
   Sew   C-1-2-3 to #4.   Press.
   Continue adding strips in order. Press.

Repeat these instructions for the remaining blocks:
   6 of Aqua-Lavender,
   6 of Lavender-Pink
   6 of Pink-Yellow and
   6 of Yellow-Green.

TIP: Each 2-Color block is named with the
   upper left corner first.
   Number the blocks as you sew them.
   • Green-Aqua (blocks 1, 10, 14, 18, 22, 26)
   • Aqua-Lavender (blocks 2, 6, 15, 19, 23, 27)
   • Lavender-Pink (blocks 3, 7, 11, 20, 24, 28)
   • Pink-Yellow (blocks 4, 8, 12, 16, 25, 29)
   • Yellow-Green (blocks 5, 9, 13, 17, 21, 30)
      (You will have 6 of each block.)

Preparation for Aqua-Lavender Blocks 2, 6, 15, 19, 23, 27:
From Aqua print strips, cut 6 each of the following:
   #1: 2½" x 2½"   #6: 2½" x 8½"
   #2: 2½" x 4½"   #9: 2½" x 10½"
   #5: 2½" x 6½"   #10: 2½" x 12½"
From Lavender print strips, cut 6 each of the following:
   #3: 2½" x 4½"   #8: 2½" x 10½"
   #4: 2½" x 6½"   #11: 2½" x 12½"
   #7: 2½" x 8½"   #12: 2½" x 14½"
(You will have 6 of each number.)

Preparation for Lavender-Pink Blocks 3, 7, 11, 20, 24, 28:
From Lavender print strips, cut 6 each of the following:
   #1: 2½" x 2½"   #6: 2½" x 8½"
   #2: 2½" x 4½"   #9: 2½" x 10½"
   #5: 2½" x 6½"   #10: 2½" x 12½"
From Pink print strips, cut 6 each of the following:
   #3: 2½" x 4½"   #8: 2½" x 10½"
   #4: 2½" x 6½"   #11: 2½" x 12½"
   #7: 2½" x 8½"   #12: 2½" x 14½"
(You will have 6 of each number.)

Preparation for Pink-Yellow Blocks 4, 8, 12, 16, 25, 29:
From Pink print strips, cut 6 each of the following:
   #1: 2½" x 2½"   #6: 2½" x 8½"
   #2: 2½" x 4½"   #9: 2½" x 10½"
   #5: 2½" x 6½"   #10: 2½" x 12½"
From Yellow print strips, cut 6 each of the following:
   #3: 2½" x 4½"   #8: 2½" x 10½"
   #4: 2½" x 6½"   #11: 2½" x 12½"
   #7: 2½" x 8½"   #12: 2½" x 14½"
(You will have 6 of each number.)

Preparation for Yellow-Green Blocks 5, 9, 13, 17, 21, 30:
From Yellow print strips, cut 6 each of the following:
   #1: 2½" x 2½"   #6: 2½" x 8½"
   #2: 2½" x 4½"   #9: 2½" x 10½"
   #5: 2½" x 6½"   #10: 2½" x 12½"
From Green print strips, cut 6 each of the following:
   #3: 2½" x 4½"   #8: 2½" x 10½"
   #4: 2½" x 6½"   #11: 2½" x 12½"
   #7: 2½" x 8½"   #12: 2½" x 14½"
(You will have 6 of each number.)

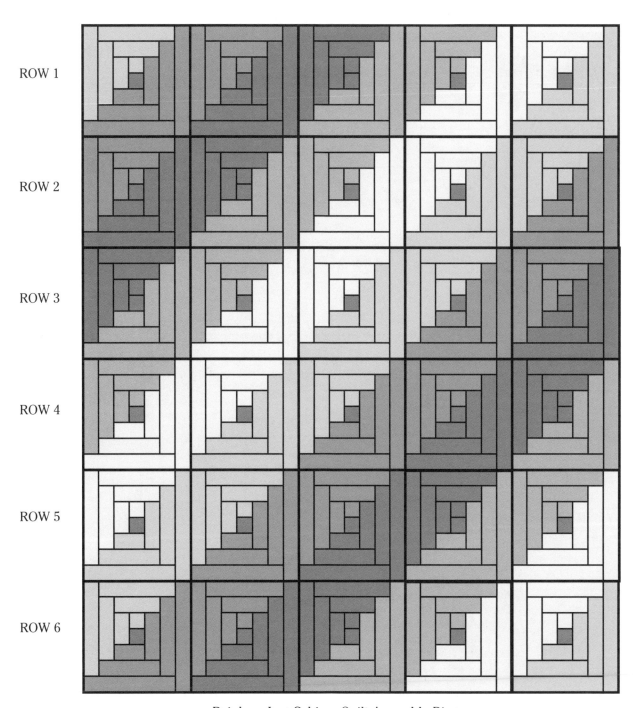

ROW 1

ROW 2

ROW 3

ROW 4

ROW 5

ROW 6

Rainbow Log Cabin - Quilt Assembly Diagram

ASSEMBLY:
Refer to diagram for block placement and direction.
Sew blocks together in 6 rows, 5 blocks per row. Press.
Sew rows together. Press.

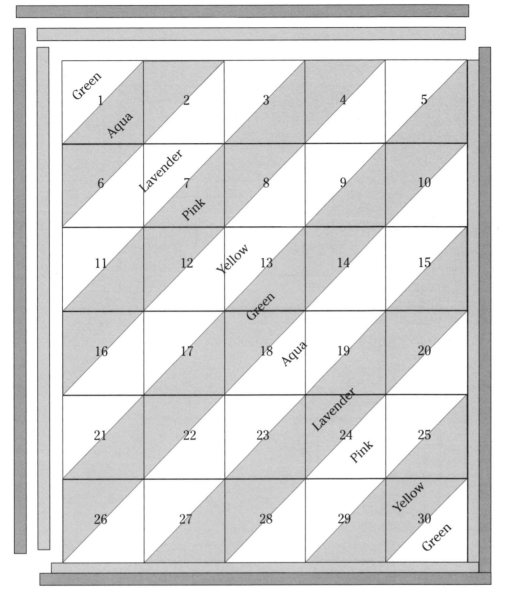

Rainbow Log Cabin - Quilt Assembly Diagram

Border #1:
Cut strips 1½" by the width of fabric.
Sew strips together end to end.
    Cut 2 strips 1½" x 84½" for sides.
    Cut 2 strips 1½" x 72½" for top and bottom.
    Sew side borders to the quilt. Press.
    Sew top and bottom borders to the quilt.
    Press.

Border #2:
Cut strips 1½" by the width of fabric.
Sew strips together end to end.
    Cut 2 strips 1½" x 86½" for sides.
    Cut 2 strips 1½" x 74½" for top and bottom.
    Sew side borders to the quilt. Press.
    Sew top and bottom borders to the quilt.
    Press.

Outer Border #3:
Cut strips 6½" wide parallel to the selvage to
eliminate piecing.
Cut 2 strips 6½" x 88½" for sides.
Cut 2 strips 6½" x 86½" for top and bottom.
Sew side borders to the quilt. Press.
Sew top and bottom borders to the quilt. Press.

FINISHING:
Quilting:
See Basic Instructions.
Binding:
Cut strips 2½" wide.
Sew together end to end to equal 382".
See Binding Instructions.

Note: This quilt is also available as a pattern pack
#0953 "Rainbow of Colors" by Design Originals.

Stairway to Heaven

photo is on page 13

SIZE: 65" x 74"

YARDAGE:
Yardage is given for using either fabric yardage or
    'Layer Cake' squares.
We used a *Moda* "Urban Couture" by Basic Grey
    'Layer Cake' collection of 10" x 10" fabric squares
    - we purchased 1 'Layer Cake'

10 squares	OR	⅞ yard Yellow
10 squares	OR	⅞ yard Blue
7 squares	OR	⅝ yard Green
6 squares	OR	⅝ yard Brown
3 squares	OR	⅓ yard Red

Border #2	Purchase ½ yard Red
Border #3 & Binding	Purchase 1⅞ yards Blue
Backing	Purchase 4 yards
Batting	Purchase 73" x 82"

Sewing machine, needle, thread

PREPARATION FOR SQUARES:
    Cut all squares 10" x 10".
    Label the stacks or pieces as you cut.

SORTING:
    Sort the following 10" x 10" squares into stacks:

POSITION	QUANTITY & COLOR	
Corner squares A	4	Yellow
Half-Square triangles B	4 Green, 4 Blue	
Half-Square triangles C	6 Yellow, 6 Blue	
Center bars D	3	Green
Center bars E	3	Red
Pieced border #1	6	Brown

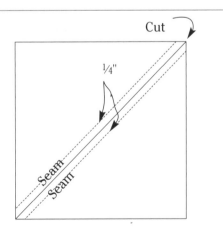

Half-Square Triangle Diagram
1. Place 2 squares right sides together.
2. Draw a diagonal line from corner to corner.
3. Stitch ¼" on each side of the line.
4. Cut squares apart on the diagonal line.
5. Open the 2 new squares with 2 colors.
6. Press. Trim off dog-ears.
7. Center and trim to size.

HALF-SQUARE TRIANGLES:
Match the following squares for the half-square triangles:
    4 pairs of Green - Blue (B)
    6 pairs of Yellow - Blue (C)
Follow the instructions in the Half-Square Triangle Diagram
    to make 20 half-square triangles; 8 B and 12 C.

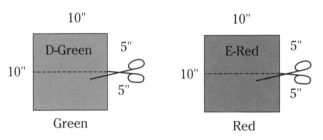

Center Bars Diagram

Cut Red and Green 10" x 10" squares in half.

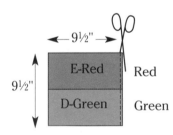

Sew Green and Red pieces together in pairs.
Trim to 9½" x 9½". Make 6.

CENTER BARS:
Cut 3 Red and 3 Green squares in half.
    Sew 6 pairs of Red-Green. Press.
    Trim to 9½" x 9½".
    Sew a strip of 3 bars: Green-Red-Green-Red-Green-Red.
Press.
    Make 2.
    Sew the strips together with 2 Red ends in the middle.
Press.
    The strip will measure 9½" x 54½".

ASSEMBLY:
    Arrange all blocks on a work surface or table.
    Refer to diagram for block placement and direction.
    Sew 4 columns, 6 blocks per column. Press.
    Sew 2 columns to the right and left sides of the Center bars. Press.

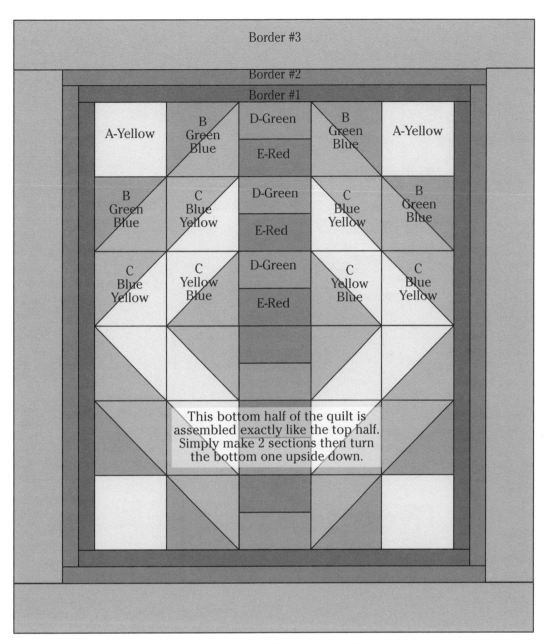

Stairway to Heaven - Quilt Assembly Diagram

BORDERS:

Pieced Border #1:
Cut strips 2½" x 10".
Sew strips together end to end.
    Cut 2 strips 2½" x 54½" for sides.
    Cut 2 strips 2½" x 49½" for top and bottom.
    Sew side borders to the quilt. Press.
    Sew top and bottom borders to the quilt. Press.

Border #2:
Cut strips 2½" by the width of fabric.
Sew strips together end to end.
    Cut 2 strips 2½" x 58½" for sides.
    Cut 2 strips 2½" x 53½" for top and bottom.
    Sew side borders to the quilt. Press.
    Sew top and bottom borders to the quilt. Press.

Outer Border #3:
Cut strips 6½" wide parallel to the selvage to
    eliminate piecing.
    Cut 2 strips 6½" x 62½" for sides.
    Cut 2 strips 6½" x 65½" for top and bottom.
    Sew side borders to the quilt. Press.
    Sew top and bottom borders to the quilt. Press.

FINISHING:
Quilting: See Basic Instructions .
Binding: Cut strips 2½" wide.
    Sew together end to end to equal 289".
    See Binding Instructions.

Five Friends

photos are on pages 14 - 15

SIZE: 62" x 74"
TIP: Add more borders to make a larger quilt.

YARDAGE:
     Yardage is given for using either fabric yardage or 'Jelly Roll' strips.
We used a *Moda* "Civil War Crossing" by Barbara Brackman
    'Jelly Roll' collection of 2½" fabric strips
    - we purchased 1 'Jelly Roll'

10 strips	OR	¾ yard Medium Brown
8 strips	OR	⅝ yard Blue
7 strips	OR	½ yard Red
6 strips	OR	½ yard Pink
4 strips	OR	⅓ yard Dark Brown
2 strips	OR	⅙ yard Navy
2 strips	OR	⅙ yard Tan

Cornerstones & Stars	Purchase 1 yard Tan
Border #1	Purchase ½ yard Red
Border #2 & Binding	Purchase 2¼ yards Brown print
Backing	Purchase 3⅞ yards
Batting	Purchase 70" x 82"

Sewing machine, needle, thread

PREPARATION FOR STRIPS:
    Cut all strips 2½" by the width of fabric (usually 42" - 44").
    Label the stacks or pieces as you cut.

SORTING:

Sort the following 2½" strips into stacks:

POSITION	QUANTITY & COLOR
Checkerboard Centers	2 Red, 3 Blue, 1 Medium Brown, 1 Pink
Star Blocks	4 Dark Brown, 4 Medium Brown, 2 Navy and Tan yardage
Patchwork Blocks	4 Medium Brown, 4 Blue, 4 Red, 4 Pink
Patchwork Borders	1 Pink, 2 Brown, 3 Blue, 2 Tan, 1 Red

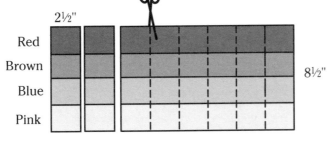

Assortment of Strips #1 - Make 1

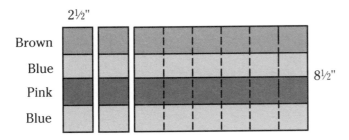

Assortment of Strips #2 - Make 1

CHECKERBOARD BLOCKS:
Centers for Blocks:
You will need
1 Red, 2 Blue, 1 Medium Brown, 1 Pink strips.

Cut the following into strips 21" long:
2 Red, 3 Blue, 2 Brown, 1 Pink

Assortment of Strips #1:
Sew the strips together side by side. Press.
Red, Brown, Blue, Pink
Cut the strip-set into 8 units 2½" x 8½".

Assortment of Strips #2:
Sew the strips together side by side. Press
Brown, Blue, Pink, Blue
Cut the strip-set into 8 units 2½" x 8½".

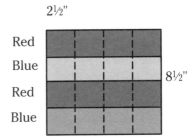

Assortment of Strips #3 - Make 1

Cut the leftovers into strips 10½" long:
2 Red, 2 Blue

Assortment of Strips #3:
Sew the strips together side by side.
Press.
Red, Blue, Red, Blue
Cut the strip-set into 4 units 2½" x 8½".

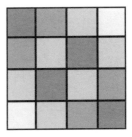

Checkerboard Block
Make 5

CHECKERBOARD CENTERS:
Make 5.
Scramble the rows of strip-sets to make scrappy checkerboard centers for each star.
Refer to the Checkerboard Block diagram.
Arrange 4 rows for each block.
Sew the rows together side by side. Press.
Each block will measure 8½" x 8½" at this point.

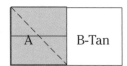 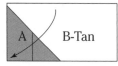

Align a square with the end of the block. Sew a diagonal line as shown. Fold back the triangle. Press.

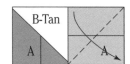 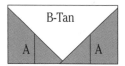

Align a square with the other end of the block. Sew a diagonal line as shown. Fold back the triangle. Press.

Flying Geese Diagram

FLYING GEESE UNITS:
Label the pieces as you cut.

Cutting for B-Tan for Star Blocks:
B   Cut 20 rectangles 4½" x 8½" from Tan yardage.

Cutting for A-Points for Star Blocks:
You will need 4 Dark Brown strips, 4 Medium Brown strips and 2 Navy strips.
Sew the strips together side by side in pairs of colors (4½" x 42").
A   Cut 40 squares 4½" x 4½" (16 Dark Brown, 16 Medium Brown, 8 Navy).
Refer to the Flying Geese Diagram to make 20 Flying Geese units.

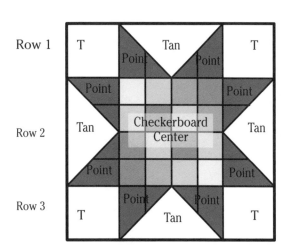

Star Block - Make 5

STAR BLOCKS:
Make 5 star blocks
    (2 with Medium Brown Points, 2 with Dark Brown Points, and 1 with Navy Points).
    Center - You will need 5 Checkerboard squares (see page 2) 8½" x 8½".

Cutting for T-Tan for Star Blocks:
T Corners   Cut 20 squares 4½" x 4½" from Tan yardage.

Assembly:
Refer to Star Block diagram for placement and direction.
    Rows 1 & 3:
        Sew a T corner - A/B/A unit - T corner. Press.
        Make 10 units (4 Dark Brown, 4 Medium Brown, and 2 Navy).
    Row 2:
        Sew an A/B/A unit - Checkerboard center - A/B/A unit. Press.
        Make 5 units (2 Dark Brown, 2 Medium Brown, and 1 Navy).
    Assembly:
        Sew the rows together. Press.
        Each block will measure 16½" x 16½" at this point.

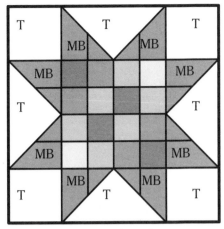

Star Block with
Medium Brown Points
Make 2

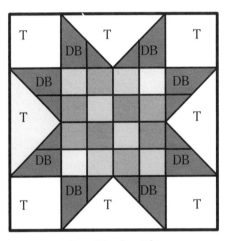

Star Block with
Dark Brown Points
Make 2

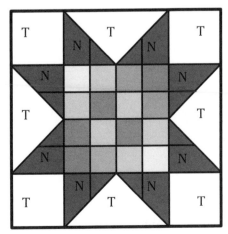

Star Block with
Navy Points
Make 1

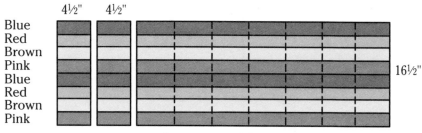

Assortment of Strips #1

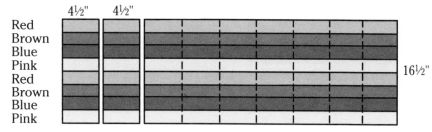

Assortment of Strips #2

PATCHWORK BLOCKS:

You will need 4 Medium Brown, 4 Blue, 4 Red, 4 Pink strips.

Cut the following into strips 42" long:
    4 Medium Brown, 4 Blue, 4 Red, 4 Pink

Assortment of Strips #1:
    Sew the strips together side by side. Press.
        Blue, Red, Brown, Pink, Blue, Red, Brown, Pink
    Cut the strip-set into 9 units, each 4½" x 16½".

Assortment of Strips #2:
    Sew the strips together side by side. Press.
        Red, Brown, Blue, Pink, Red, Brown, Blue, Pink
    Cut the strip-set into 9 units, each 4½" x 16½".

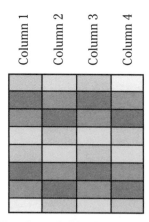

Patchwork Block Assembly

PATCHWORK BLOCKS:

Make 4.
Scramble the rows of strip-sets to make scrappy patchwork blocks.
    Refer to the diagram.
Arrange 4 columns for each block.
Sew the columns together side by side. Press.
Each block will measure 16½" x 16½" at this point.

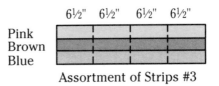

Pink
Brown
Blue

6½" 6½" 6½" 6½"

Assortment of Strips #3

Tan
Brown
Blue

4½" 4½" 4½" 4½" 4½" 4½" 4½" 4½"

Assortment of Strips #4

Red
Blue
Tan

6½" 6½" 6½" 6½" 8½" 8½"

Assortment of Strips #5

PATCHWORK BORDERS -TOP & BOTTOM:

You will need 1 Pink, 2 Brown, 3 Blue, 2 Tan, 1 Red strips. Sort strips into the 3 groups below.

Assortment of Strips #3:
Cut the following into strips 27" long:
1 Pink, 1 Brown, 1 Blue
Sew the strips together side by side. Press.
Cut the strip-set into 4 units, each 6½" x 6½".

Assortment of Strips #4:
Cut the following into strips 37" long:
1 Blue, 1 Brown, 1 Tan
Sew the strips together side by side. Press.
Cut the strip-set into 8 units, each 6½" x 4½".

Assortment of Strips #5:
Cut the following into strips 43" long:
1 Red, 1 Blue, 1 Tan
Sew the strips together side by side. Press.
Cut the strip-set into units:
4 units, each 6½" x 6½" and
2 units, each 6½" x 8½".

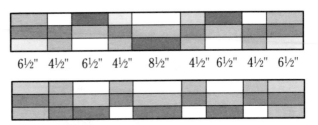

6½" 4½" 6½" 4½" 8½"   4½" 6½" 4½" 6½"

TOP AND BOTTOM BORDERS

Scramble the rows of strip-sets to make scrappy borders. Refer to the diagram.
Sew the columns together side by side. Press.
Each border will measure 6½" x 48½" at this point.

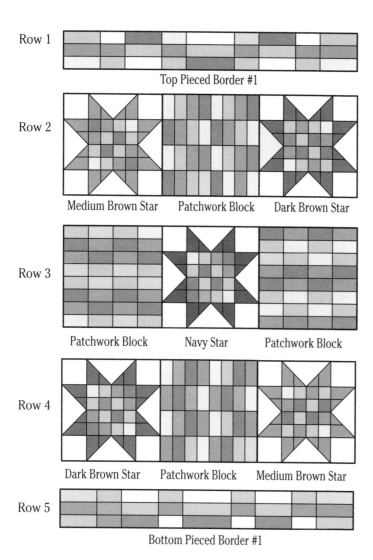

Row 1

Top Pieced Border #1

Row 2

Medium Brown Star   Patchwork Block   Dark Brown Star

Row 3

Patchwork Block   Navy Star   Patchwork Block

Row 4

Dark Brown Star   Patchwork Block   Medium Brown Star

Row 5

Bottom Pieced Border #1

ASSEMBLY:

    Arrange all blocks on a work surface or table.
    Refer to diagram for block placement and direction.
    Sew blocks together in 3 rows, 3 blocks per row. Press.
    Position top and bottom borders as rows 1 and 5.
    Sew rows together. Press.

Mitered Border

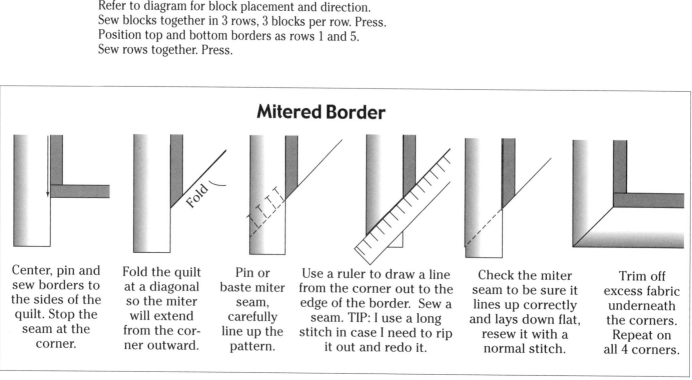

Center, pin and sew borders to the sides of the quilt. Stop the seam at the corner.

Fold the quilt at a diagonal so the miter will extend from the corner outward.

Pin or baste miter seam, carefully line up the pattern.

Use a ruler to draw a line from the corner out to the edge of the border. Sew a seam. TIP: I use a long stitch in case I need to rip it out and redo it.

Check the miter seam to be sure it lines up correctly and lays down flat, resew it with a normal stitch.

Trim off excess fabric underneath the corners. Repeat on all 4 corners.

Five Friends - Quilt Assembly

BORDERS:

Inner Border #1:
Cut strips 2½" by the width of fabric.
Sew strips together end to end.

Cut 2 strips 2½" x 60½" for sides.
Cut 2 strips 2½" x 52½" for top and bottom.
Sew side borders to the quilt. Press.
Sew top and bottom borders to the quilt.
Press.

Mitered Outer Border #2:
The border print we used is 5" wide. Adjust these measurements to accommodate the width of your chosen border.

Center, pin, and sew 5½" x 78½" borders to the sides of the quilt. Press.

Center, pin, and sew 5½" x 66½" borders to the top and bottom of the quilt. Press.

Miter the corners.

See the Basic Instructions for Mitered Borders. Press.

FINISHING:

Quilting: See Basic Instructions.
Binding: Cut strips 2½" wide.
Sew together end to end to equal 282".
See Binding Instructions.

Note: This quilt is also available as a pattern pack #0954 "Five Friends" by Design Originals.

Kaleidoscope of Color

photo is on pages 16 - 17

SIZE: 44" x 60"
TIP: Add more borders to make a larger quilt.

YARDAGE:
Yardage is given for using either fabric yardage or
'Layer Cake' squares.
We used a *Moda* "Charisma" by Chez Moi
   'Layer Cake' collection of 10" x 10" fabric squares
   - we purchased 1 'Layer Cake'

2 squares	OR	⅓ yard Green
3 squares	OR	⅓ yard Pink
3 squares	OR	⅓ yard Blue/Green
3 squares	OR	⅓ yard Red print
4 squares	OR	⅓ yard Dark Blue
4 squares	OR	⅓ yard Light Blue
4 squares	OR	⅓ yard Red

Border #1	Purchase ⅜ yard Brown
Border #2 & Binding	Purchase 1½ yards of Blue-Green print
Backing	Purchase 2½ yards
Batting	Purchase 52" x 68"

Sewing machine, needle, thread

SMALLER BONUS QUILT:

Border #1	Purchase ½ yard Brown
Border #2 & Binding	Purchase 1 yard Blue-Green print
Backing	Purchase 1⅓ yards
Batting	Purchase 44" x44"

PREPARATION FOR SQUARES:
   Cut all Layer Cake squares into 4 squares 5" x 5".
   From Brown fabric for Border #1,
   cut 12 squares 5" x 5".

SORTING:
   Sort and label the following 5" x 5" squares:

POSITION	QUANTITY & COLOR	
A	4 Green	4 Pink
B	4 Green	4 Blue/Green
C	6 Blue/Green	6 Dark Blue
D	6 Dark Blue	6 Light Blue
E	2 Dark Blue	2 Brown
F	6 Light Blue	6 Red
G	2 Light Blue	2 Brown
H	2 Red	2 Brown
I	6 Red	6 Red print
J	2 Red print	2 Brown
K	4 Red print	4 Pink
L	2 Pink	2 Brown
M	2 Blue/Green	2 Brown

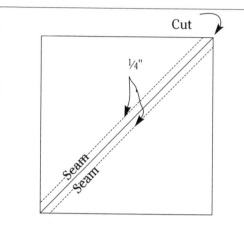

Half-Square Triangle Diagram
1. Place 2 squares right sides together.
2. Draw a diagonal line from corner to corner.
3. Stitch ¼" on each side of the line.
4. Cut squares apart on the diagonal line.
5. Open the 2 new squares with 2 colors.
6. Press. Trim off dog-ears.
7. Center and trim to size.

HALF-SQUARE TRIANGLES:
Match the following squares for the
   half-square triangles:

A	4 pairs of	Green - Pink
B	4 pairs of	Green - Blue/Green
C	6 pairs of	Blue/Green - Dark Blue
D	6 pairs of	Dark Blue - Light Blue
E	2 pairs of	Dark Blue - Brown
F	6 pairs of	Light Blue - Red
G	2 pairs of	Light Blue - Brown
H	2 pairs of	Red - Brown
I	6 pairs of	Red - Red print
J	2 pairs of	Red print - Brown
K	4 pairs of	Red print - Pink
L	2 pairs of	Pink - Brown
M	2 pairs of	Blue/Green - Brown

Follow the instructions in the Half-Square
   Triangle Diagram to make 96 half-square
   triangles. Trim to 4½" x 4½".

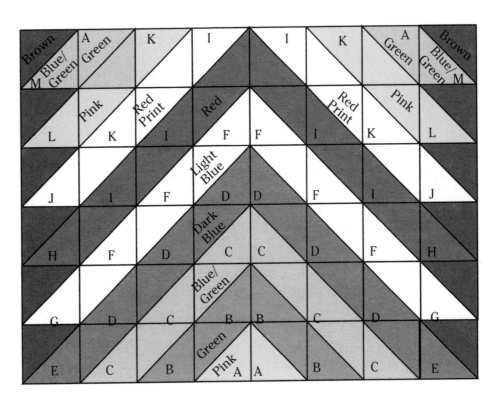

Kaleidoscope of Color - Quilt Assembly Diagram
Make 2 for top and bottom of the Quilt

ASSEMBLY:

Arrange all blocks on a work surface or table.

Refer to the large Quilt Assembly diagram for block placement and direction.

Sew blocks together in 12 rows (you'll have 2 rows of each), 8 blocks per row. Press.

Sew 2 sets of 6 rows together. Make one for the top section and one for the bottom section.

Sew the sections together. Press.

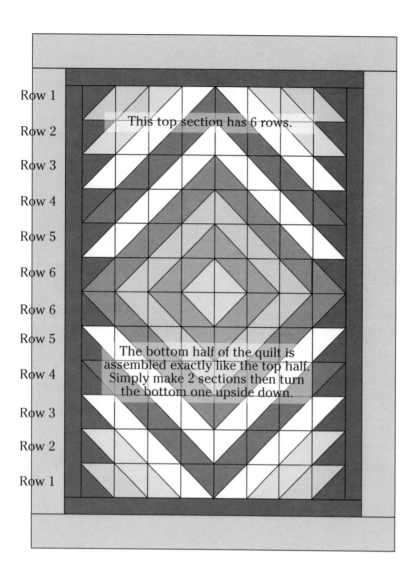

Row 1
Row 2
Row 3
Row 4
Row 5
Row 6
Row 6
Row 5
Row 4
Row 3
Row 2
Row 1

This top section has 6 rows.

The bottom half of the quilt is assembled exactly like the top half. Simply make 2 sections then turn the bottom one upside down.

BORDERS

Refer to the large Assembly diagram.

Border #1:

Cut strips 2½" by the width of fabric.

Sew strips together end to end.

Cut 2 strips 2½" x 48½" for sides.

Cut 2 strips 2½" x 36½" for top and bottom.

Sew side borders to the quilt. Press.

Sew top and bottom borders to the quilt. Press.

Outer Border #2:

Cut strips 4½" wide parallel to the selvage to eliminate piecing.

Cut 2 strips 4½" x 52½" for sides.

Cut 2 strips 4½" x 44½" for top and bottom.

Sew side borders to the quilt. Press.

Sew top and bottom borders to the quilt. Press.

FINISHING:

Quilting: See Basic Instructions.

Binding: Cut strips 2½" wide.

Sew together end to end to equal 218".

See Binding Instructions.

Note: This quilt is also available as a pattern pack

0959 "Kaleidoscope of Color" by Design Originals.

Kaleidoscope of Color - Quilt Assembly Diagram

Small Kaleidoscope

photo is on page 16

SIZE: 36" x 36"

TIP: Add more borders to make a larger quilt.

YARDAGE:
We used a *Moda* "Charisma" by Chez Moi
    'Layer Cake' collection of 10" x 10" fabric squares
    - we purchased 1 'Layer Cake'
    (We used the leftover squares from the large
       Kaleidoscope of Color quilt.)

2 squares	OR	⅓ yard Light Blue
2 squares	OR	⅓ yard Ivory
2 squares	OR	⅓ yard Stripe
2 squares	OR	⅓ yard Pink

Border #1   Purchase ½ yard Brown
Border #2 & Binding   Purchase 1⅛ yard Blue-Green print
Backing   Purchase 1⅓ yards
Batting   Purchase 44" x44"
Sewing machine, needle, thread

PREPARATION FOR SQUARES:
    Cut all Layer Cake squares into 4 squares 5" x 5".
    From Brown fabric for Border #1, cut 10 squares 5" x 5".

SORTING:
    Sort, cut and label the following 5" x 5" squares:

POSITION	QUANTITY & COLOR
A	6 Ivory, 6 Light Blue
B	2 Ivory, 2 Stripe
C	6 Pink, 6 Brown
D	4 Stripe, 4 Brown

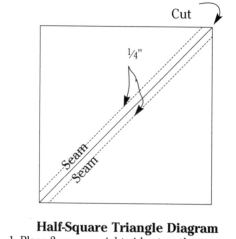

Half-Square Triangle Diagram
1. Place 2 squares right sides together.
2. Draw a diagonal line from corner to corner.
3. Stitch ¼" on each side of the line.
4. Cut squares apart on the diagonal line.
5. Open the 2 new squares with 2 colors.
6. Press. Trim off dog-ears.
7. Center and trim to size.

HALF-SQUARE TRIANGLES:
Pair up the following squares for the half-square
       triangles:
    A   6 pairs of Ivory - Light Blue
    B   2 pairs of Ivory - Stripe
    C   6 pairs of Pink - Brown
    D   4 pairs of Stripe-Brown
Follow the instructions in the Half-Square
    Triangle Diagram.
Make 36 half-square triangles.
    Trim to 4½" x 4½".

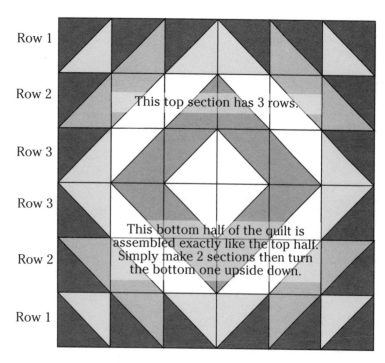

Row 1

Row 2 — This top section has 3 rows.

Row 3

Row 3

Row 2 — This bottom half of the quilt is assembled exactly like the top half. Simply make 2 sections then turn the bottom one upside down.

Row 1

ASSEMBLY:
Arrange all blocks on a work surface or
    table.
Refer to the Quilt Assembly diagram
    for block placement and direction.
Sew blocks together in 6 rows
    (you'll have 2 rows of each),
    6 blocks per row. Press.

Sew 2 sets of 3 rows together.
Make one for the top section and
    one for the bottom section.
Sew the sections together.
    Press.

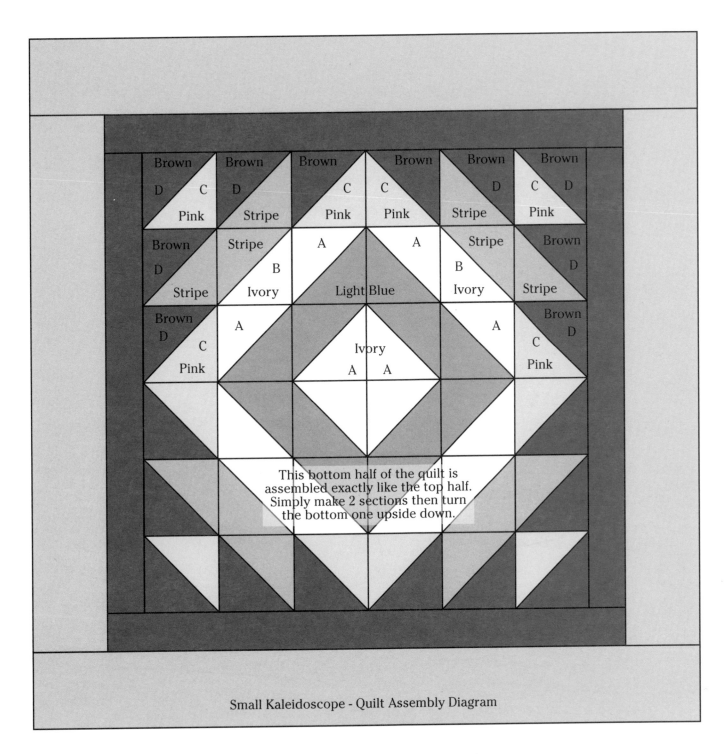

Small Kaleidoscope - Quilt Assembly Diagram

BORDERS:

Border #1:
Cut strips 2½" by the width of fabric.
Sew strips together end to end.
    Cut 2 strips 2½" x 24½" for sides.
    Cut 2 strips 2½" x 28½" for top and bottom.
    Sew side borders to the quilt. Press.
    Sew top and bottom borders to the quilt. Press.

Outer Border #2:
Cut strips 4½" wide parallel to the selvage to
    eliminate piecing.
    Cut 2 strips 4½" x 28½" for sides.
    Cut 2 strips 4½" x 36½" for top and bottom.
    Sew side borders to the quilt. Press.
    Sew top and bottom borders to the quilt. Press.

FINISHING:
Quilting: See Basic Instructions.
Binding: Cut strips 2½" wide.
    Sew together end to end to equal 154".
    See Binding Instructions.

Note: This quilt is also available as a pattern pack
    0959 "Kaleidoscope of Color" by Design Originals.

Tree
Cut 1 Stripe

Add a scant 1/4" around the
edge for turned applique

Join Tree sections here.

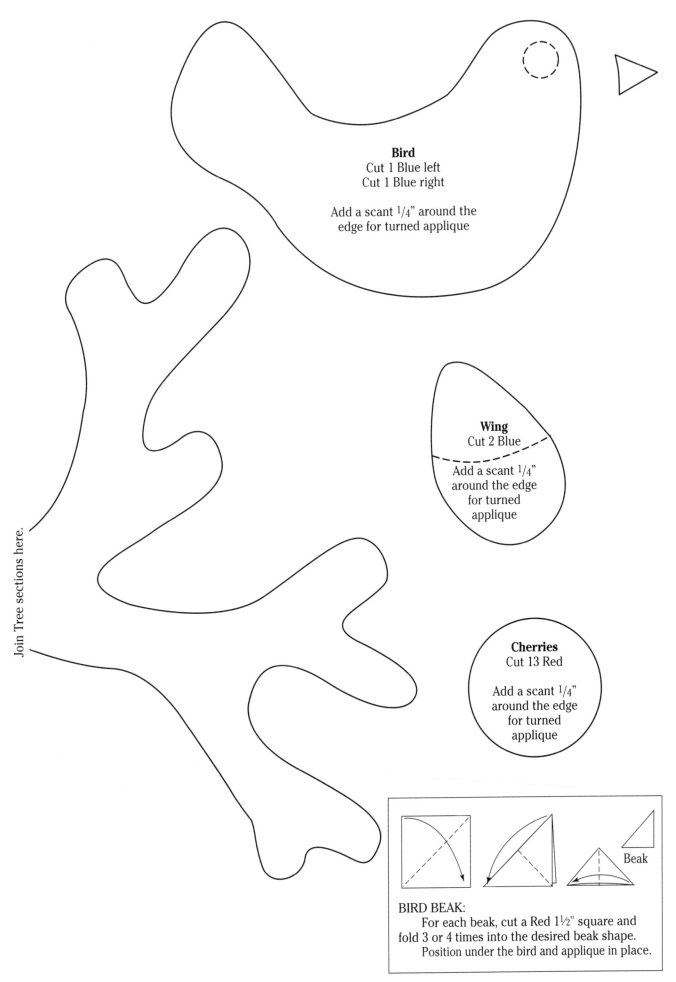

Bird
Cut 1 Blue left
Cut 1 Blue right

Add a scant 1/4" around the
edge for turned applique

Wing
Cut 2 Blue

Add a scant 1/4"
around the edge
for turned
applique

Cherries
Cut 13 Red

Add a scant 1/4"
around the edge
for turned
applique

Join Tree sections here.

Beak

BIRD BEAK:
   For each beak, cut a Red 1½" square and
fold 3 or 4 times into the desired beak shape.
   Position under the bird and applique in place.

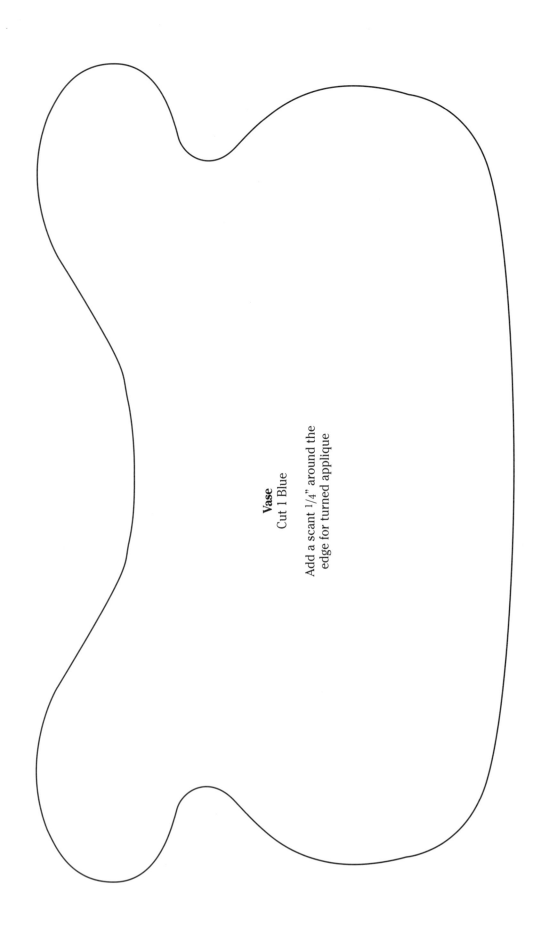

Vase
Cut 1 Blue

Add a scant 1/4" around the
edge for turned applique

Tree of Life

photo on page 83

SIZE: 38" x 46"

YARDAGE:

Yardage is given for using either fabric yardage or
'Jelly Roll' strips.
We used a *Moda* "Charisma" by Chez Moi
'Jelly Roll' collection of 2½" fabric strips
- we purchased 1 'Jelly Roll'

3 strips	OR	¼ yard Blue-Green print
2 strips	OR	⅙ yard Brown
2 strips	OR	⅙ yard Stripe
1 strip	OR	⅛ yard Pink
1 strip	OR	⅛ yard Red

Center A	Purchase ½ yard Ivory
Border #5 & Squares C	Purchase ⅓ yard Green
Applique, Border #6 & Binding	Purchase 1⅓ yards Stripe
Applique	Purchase ⅙ yard Blue
Backing	Purchase 1¾ yards
Batting	Purchase 46" x 54"

Sewing machine, needle, thread
DMC pearl cotton or 6-ply floss
#22 or #24 chenille needle

PREPARATION FOR STRIPS:

Cut all strips 2½" by the width of fabric
(usually 42" - 44").
Label the stacks or pieces as you cut.

SORTING:

Sort the following 2½" strips into stacks:

POSITION	QUANTITY & COLOR	
Border 1	1	Brown
Border 2	2	Stripes
Border 3	1	Pink, 1 Brown, 1 Red
Border 4	3	Blue-Green print

CUTTING:

Cut 1 Ivory center 13" x 21".
Cut 12 Green C squares 2½" x 2½".

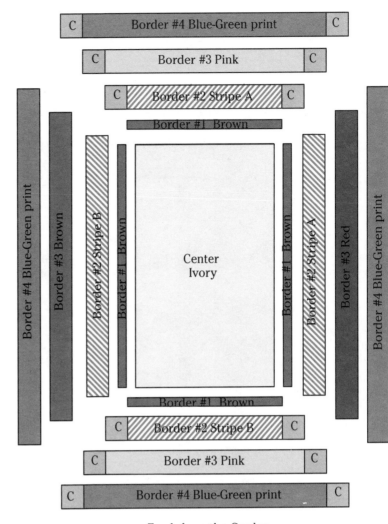

Fresh from the Garden
Border Assembly Diagram

BORDER

Border #1:
Cut 1 Brown strip in half to make 2 pieces 1¼" x 42.
Sew strips together end to end.
    Cut 2 strips 1¼" x 21" for sides.
    Cut 2 strips 1¼" x 14½" for top and bottom.
    Sew side borders to the quilt. Press.
    Sew top and bottom borders to the quilt. Press.

Border #2:
Cut 2 different Stripes, A and B, 2½" by the width of fabric.
Sew strips together end to end.
    Cut 1 A and 1 B Stripe 2½" x 22½" for sides.
    Cut 1 A and 1 B Stripe 2½" x 14½" for top and bottom.
    Sew side borders to the quilt. Press.
    Sew a C square to each end of top and bottom strips.
    Sew top and bottom borders to the quilt. Press.

Border #3:
    Cut 1 Brown and 1 Red strip 2½" x 26½" for sides.
    Cut 2 Pink strips 2½" x 18½" for top and bottom.
    Sew side borders to the quilt. Press.
    Sew a C square to each end of top and bottom strips.
    Sew top and bottom borders to the quilt. Press.

Border #4:
    Cut 2 Blue-Green strips 2½" x 30½" for sides.
    Cut 2 Blue-Green strips 2½" x 22½" for top and bottom.
    Sew side borders to the quilt. Press.
    Sew a C square to each end of top and bottom strips.
    Sew top and bottom borders to the quilt. Press.

Tree of Life - Quilt Assembly Diagram

BORDERS:

Border #5:

Cut 2 strips 2½" x 34½" for sides.
Cut 2 strips 2½" x 30½" for top and bottom.
Sew side borders to the quilt. Press.
Sew top and bottom borders to the quilt. Press.

Mitered Border #6:

Cut strips 4½" wide parallel to the selvage to
eliminate piecing.
Cut 2 strips 4½" x 50½" for sides.
Cut 2 strips 4½" x 42½" for top and bottom.
Refer to the Basic Instructions for Mitered Borders.

Applique: See Basic Instructions.

Cut out shapes from patterns. Applique as desired.
For bird beaks, cut a Red 1½" square. Fold it 3 or 4
times into a beak shape.
Position under the bird body and applique in place.

FINISHING:

Quilting: See Basic Instructions.

Binding: Cut strips 2½" wide.
Sew together end to end to equal 178".
See Binding Instructions.

Suppliers - Most quilt and fabric stores carry an excellent assortment of supplies. If you need something special, ask your local store to contact the following companies.

FABRICS, 'JELLY ROLLS',
'FAT QUARTERS'
   Moda and United Notions,
   Dallas, TX, 972-484-8901

QUILTERS
   Susan Corbett, 817-361-7762
   Julie Lawson, 817-428-5929
   Sue Needle, 817-589-1168

MANY THANKS
to my staff for
their cheerful
help and wonder-
ful ideas!
Kathy Mason
Patty Williams
Donna Kinsey
Janet Long
David & Donna
Thomason